D1463901

000048620

Readings in Literary Criticism 2

CRITICS ON
CHARLOTTE AND EMILY BRONTË

Readings in Literary Criticism

CRITICS ON CHARLOTTE AND EMILY BRONTË

Readings in Literary Criticism

Edited by Judith O'Neill

London
GEORGE ALLEN & UNWIN
Boston   Sydney

FIRST PUBLISHED IN 1968
SECOND IMPRESSION 1971
THIRD IMPRESSION 1977

This anthology © George Allen & Unwin (Publishers) Ltd, 1968

ISBN 0 04 801005 7

PRINTED IN GREAT BRITAIN BY
COX & WYMAN LTD, LONDON, FAKENHAM AND READING

INTRODUCTION

They were sisters but they were not alike, either as women or as writers. When we read on from *Jane Eyre* and *Villette* to the Gondal poems and *Wuthering Heights,* we move into a different world. Sydney Dobell, one of the first critics to write about the Brontës, recognized this sharp distinction when he reviewed the *Poems* by C., E., and A. Bell in 1846. Before any of the novels had been written, Dobell realized that E[mily]'s poems stood apart from those of her sisters (or, as he thought, brothers), and that she had a 'fine quaint spirit' with a remarkable power as yet untried. Seventy years later, in 1916, Virginia Woolf was making much the same point in her discussion of *Jane Eyre* and *Wuthering Heights.* Between those two dates, most critics had leant the other way in preferring Charlotte's more simple certainties to Emily's wild and puzzling questions. Virginia Woolf's essay was the beginning of a decisive swing in critical and popular taste that has restored the balance in Emily's favour.

Nevertheless, although they are not in the same class as *Wuthering Heights,* Charlotte Brontë's novels are worth taking seriously. Lord David Cecil is merciless to her faults but in spite of them all he is certain of her creative imaginative power: 'Out of her improbabilities and her absurdities, she constructed an original vision of life.' Kathleen Tillotson confirms this view in her study of the remarkable and conscious consistency of the characterization of Jane Eyre as a child and as an adult.

The modern critics on Charlotte Brontë are particularly interesting in two ways, apart from this sensitive attention they give to *Jane Eyre.* First, they help us to look again at *Villette* and to rescue it from an undeserved neglect. *Villette* emerges as a strikingly uneven novel but one in which the slowly maturing relationship between Lucy and Monsieur Paul has a subtlety and depth that Charlotte Brontë never managed with Jane and Rochester. And second, these critics show up, quite unconsciously, how perceptive and sympathetic was G. H. Lewes (George Eliot's husband in all but the law), writing his reviews of Charlotte Brontë's novels in the 1850's. He grasped almost all the important critical issues raised by these novels as he read the first copies straight from the press. Later critics, of course, have worked over the same issues in much greater detail, but Lewes's reviews are still well worth reading, not as museum pieces, but for their fresh and intelligent appraisal of the novels.

C. P. Sanger was not a literary critic by profession at all. He was a

Chancery barrister. But his essay on the structure of *Wuthering Heights*, published in 1921, marks a turning point in the discussion of this novel. He worked on the book like a detective, tracing clues here and there and fitting dates together, until he had laid bare the remarkable precision and accuracy of Emily Brontë's chronology and legal knowledge. He showed, once and for all, that *Wuthering Heights* was not, as it was often thought to be, the wild and random outpourings of a passionate and even unpleasant woman. The novel began to be seen as a finely controlled work of art. The critics who wrote after 1921, whether they were chiefly concerned with style or personal relationships or themes in the novel, all owe a good deal to Sanger's re-orientation.

The other landmark in the critical understanding of Emily Brontë was Fanny Ratchford's work in Texas on the Gondal manuscripts, together with C. W. Hatfield's edition of the poems in 1941. Fanny Ratchford's books were published in 1941 and 1955. Now it became possible to look at *Wuthering Heights* in the light of the Gondal saga and to relate the underlying themes of the novel and the poems. Mary Visick has profited from this research and her discussion of *Wuthering Heights* is a good place for the student to begin his own thinking about the novel, especially if he can manage to find a copy of the *Poems* as well. Mary Visick sees *Wuthering Heights* as a radical reworking of the spiritual experience that had first found expression in the poems and J. Hillis Miller, who also links the themes of poems and novel, goes on to ask some fundamental questions about the nature of the relationship between Cathy and Heathcliff and about Heathcliff's long sadistic revenge. Wade Thompson's interest in this revenge motif is primarily a psychological one. These two critics ask rather different questions about the same evidence in *Wuthering Heights* and it is worth allowing their essays to complement each other.

On the central relationship between Cathy and Heathcliff, Boris Ford and Vincent Buckley argue quite differently from each other, but for both of them certain key speeches in the novel soon stand out as crucial to any understanding of this relationship. We are driven back to the novel again to listen with sharpened awareness to Cathy's and Heathcliff's own understanding of themselves. These two critics, like Irene Cooper-Willis in her pioneering essay of 1936 (written to refute the view that the novel was the work of Emily's brother Branwell) and Mark Schorer in his discussion of metaphor, are particularly concerned with Emily Brontë's style. Vincent Buckley contrasts the staple prose of the book with the imaginative and lyrical prose of the great speeches, and once again the Gondal saga becomes relevant with its alternation of plain narrative (now lost) and the personal dramatic poems.

Jane Eyre and *Villette* may certainly be read with pleasure more than once, but *Wuthering Heights* is a book to return to again and again, an elusive and powerful tragedy that we never completely understand. The critics can help us, of course, but it is the mark of a good critic that in the end he leads us back to the novel itself and leaves us there to make our own response and our own judgment.

Cambridge, 1967

Judith O'Neill

CONTENTS

Critics on Charlotte Brontë

G. H. LEWES AND LADY EASTLAKE

The Early Reviews

Jane Eyre

Decidedly the best novel of the season; and one, moreover, from the natural tone pervading the narrative, and the originality and freshness of its style, possessing the merit so rarely met with now-a-days in works of this class, of amply repaying a second perusal. Whoever may be the author, we hope to see more such books from *her* pen; for that these volumes are from the pen of a lady, and a clever one too, we have not the shadow of a doubt: nor can there be any question as to the *reality* of many of the scenes and personages so artistically depicted; the characters are too life-like to be the mere creations of fancy, and sketchy as some of them are, they are wondrous *telling*: several of them we almost feel persuaded we have met with in real life. The Rev. Mr. Brocklehurst, with his 'straight, narrow, sable-clad shape, standing erect on the rug; the grim face at the top being like a carved mask, placed above the shaft by way of capital;' the lady-like Miss Temple; sweet Helen Burns, whose death-scene is so touchingly narrated; the neat and prim little Mrs Fairfax, and the eccentric Mr Rochester, whom with all his faults and eccentricities one can't help getting to like; are but a few of the characters in the drama, though essential ones, and cleverly struck off.

G. H. Lewes, *Westminster Review,* vol. XLVIII, 1848,
pp. 581–4.

[The page numbers in this and in all following footnotes refer to the beginning and end of the *whole* essay, article, review or chapter from which the extract is taken. The only exceptions to this practice are in the four cases of very short books or pamphlets on *Wuthering Heights* (C. P. Sanger, I. Cooper-Willis, J. F. Goodridge, Mary Visick) where the page numbers in the footnotes refer to the pages of the actual extracts.]

Since the publication of *Grantley Manor,* no novel has created so much sensation as *Jane Eyre.* Indeed, the public taste seems to have outstripped its guides in appreciating the remarkable power which this book displays. For no leading review has yet noticed it, and here we have before us the second edition. The name and sex of the writer are still a mystery. Currer Bell ... is a mere *nom de guerre*— perhaps an anagram. However, we, for our part, cannot doubt that the book is written by a female, and, as certain provincialisms indicate, by one from the North of England. Who, indeed, but a woman could have ventured, with the smallest prospect of success, to fill three octavo volumes with the history of a woman's heart? ... Yet we cannot wonder that the hypothesis of a male author should have been started, or that ladies especially should still be rather determined to uphold it. For a book more unfeminine, both in its excellences and defects, it would be hard to find in the annals of female authorship. Throughout there is masculine power, breadth and shrewdness, combined with masculine hardness, coarseness, and freedom of expression. Slang is not rare. The humour is frequently produced by a use of Scripture, at which one is rather sorry to have smiled. The love-scenes glow with a fire as fierce as that of Sappho, and somewhat more fuliginous. There is an intimate acquaintance with the worst parts of human nature, a practised sagacity in discovering the latent ulcer, and a ruthless rigour in exposing it, which must command our admiration, but are almost startling in one of the softer sex. ...

The plot is most extravagantly improbable, verging all along upon the supernatural, and at last running fairly into it. All the power is shown and all the interest lies in the characters. We have before intimated our belief, that in Jane Eyre, the heroine of the piece, we have, in some measure, a portrait of the writer. If not, it is a most skilful imitation of autobiography. The character embodied in it is precisely the same as that which pervades the whole book, and breaks out most signally in the Preface—a temper naturally harsh, made harsher by ill usage, and visiting both its defect and its wrongs upon the world—an understanding disturbed and perverted by cynicism, but still strong and penetrating—fierce love and fiercer hate—all this viewed from within and coloured by self-love. We only wish we could carry our hypothesis a step further, and suppose that the triumph which the loving and loveable element finally obtains over the unloving and unloveable in the fictitious character had also its parallel in the true. But we fear that few readers will rise from the book with that impression. ...

Anon, *Christian Remembrancer,* vol. XV, 1848, pp. 396–409.

... Altogether the auto-biography of *Jane Eyre* is pre-eminently an anti-Christian composition. There is throughout it a murmuring against the comforts of the rich and against the privations of the poor, which, as far as each individual is concerned, is a murmuring against God's appointment—there is a proud and perpetual assertion of the rights of man, for which we find no authority either in God's word or in God's providence—there is that pervading tone of ungodly discontent which is at once the most prominent and the most subtle evil which the law and the pulpit, which all civilized society in fact has at the present day to contend with. We do not hesitate to say that the tone of mind and thought which has overthrown authority and violated every code human and divine abroad, and fostered Chartism and rebellion at home, is the same which has also written *Jane Eyre*. ...

E. Rigby (Lady Eastlake), Quarterly Review,
vol. LXXXIV, 1848, pp. 173-4.

Shirley

... We take Currer Bell to be one of the most remarkable of *female* writers; and believe it is now scarcely a secret that Currer Bell is the pseudonym of a woman. ... This question of authorship, which was somewhat hotly debated a little while ago, helped to keep up the excitement about *Jane Eyre*; but, independently of that title to notoriety, it is certain that, for many years, there had been no work of such power, piquancy, and originality. Its very faults were faults on the side of vigour; and its beauties were all original. The grand secret of its success, however,—as of all genuine and lasting success,—was its *reality*. From out the depths of a sorrowing experience, here was a voice speaking to the experience of thousands. The aspects of external nature, too, were painted with equal fidelity,—the long cheerless winter days, chilled with rolling mists occasionally gathering into the strength of rains,—the bright spring mornings,—the clear solemn nights,—were all painted to your *soul* as well as to your eye, by a pencil dipped into a soul's experience for its colours. Faults enough the book has undoubtedly: faults of conception, faults of taste, faults of ignorance, but in spite of all, it remains a book of singular fascination. A more masculine book, in the sense of vigour, was never written. Indeed that vigour often amounts to coarseness,—and is certainly the very antipode to 'lady like'.

This same over-masculine vigour is even more prominent in *Shirley*, and does not increase the pleasantness of the book. A pleasant book, indeed, we are not sure that we can style it. Power it has unquestionably, and interest too, of a peculiar sort; but not the agreeableness of a work of art. Through its pages we are carried as over a wild and desolate heath, with a sharp east wind blowing the hair into our eyes, and making the blood tingle in our veins: There is health perhaps in the drive; but not much pleasantness. Nature speaks to us distinctly enough, but she does not speak sweetly. She is in her stern and sombre mood, and we see only her dreary aspects.

Shirley is inferior to *Jane Eyre* in several important points. It is not quite so true; and it is not so fascinating. It does not so rivet the reader's attention, nor hurry him through all obstacles of improbability, with so keen a sympathy in its reality. It is even coarser in texture, too, and not unfrequently flippant; while the characters are almost all disagreeable, and exhibit intolerable rudeness of manner. In *Jane Eyre* life was viewed from the standing point of individual experience; in *Shirley* that standing point is frequently abandoned, and the artist paints only a panorama of which she, as well as you, are but spectators. Hence the unity of *Jane Eyre* in spite of its clumsy and improbable contrivances, was great and effective: the fire of one passion fused the discordant materials into one mould. But in *Shirley* all unity, in consequence of defective art, is wanting. There is no passionate link; nor is there any artistic fusion, or intergrowth, by which one part evolves itself from another. Hence its falling-off in interest, coherent movement, and life. The book may be laid down at any chapter, and almost any chapter might be omitted. The various scenes are gathered up into three volumes,—they have not grown into a work. . . .

Again we say that *Shirley* cannot be received as a work of art. It is not a picture; but a portfolio of random sketches for one or more pictures. The authoress never seems distinctly to have made up her mind as to what she was to do; whether to describe the habits and manners of Yorkshire and its social aspects in the days of King Lud, or to paint character, or to tell a love story. All are by turns attempted and abandoned; and the book consequently moves slowly, and by starts—leaving behind it no distinct or satisfactory impression. Power is stamped on various parts of it; power unmistakeable, but often misapplied. Currer Bell has much yet to learn,—and, especially, the discipline of her own tumultuous energies. She must learn also to sacrifice a little of her Yorkshire roughness to the demands of good taste: neither saturating her writings with such rudeness and offensive harshness, nor suffering her style to wander into such vulgarities as would be inexcusable—even in a man. No good critic will object to the homeliness of natural diction, or to the racy flavour of conversation idiom; but every one must object to such phrases as 'Miss Mary, *getting up the steam* in her turn, now asked,' etc., or as 'making hard-handed worsted spinners *cash up to the tune of* four or five hundred per cent.,' or as 'Malone much chagrined at hearing him *pipe up in most superior style'*; all which phrases occur within the space of about a dozen pages, and that not in dialogue, but in the authoress's own narrative. . . .

We scarcely know what to say to the impertinence which has been allowed to mingle so largely with the manners, even of the favourite actors in this drama. Their frequent harshness and rudeness is something which startles on a first reading, and, on a second, is quite inexplicable. . . . The manner and language of Shirley towards her guardian passes all permission. Even the gentle, timid, shrinking Caroline enters the lists with the odious Mrs Yorke, and the two *ladies* talk at each other, in a style which, to southern ears, sounds both marvellous and alarming. But, to quit this tone of remonstrance, —which after all is a compliment, for it shows how seriously we treat the great talents of the writer,—let us cordially praise the real freshness, vividness, and fidelity, with which most of the characters and scenes are depicted. . . . Shirley, if she did not occasionally use language one would rather not hear from the lips of a lady, and did not occasion-ally display something in her behaviour, which, with every allowance for Yorkshire plainness, does imply want of breeding,—Shirley, we say, would be irresistible. So buoyant, free, airy and healthy in her nature, so fascinating in her manner, she is prettily enough described by her lover as a 'Peri too mutinous for heaven, too innocent for hell'. But if Shirley is, on the whole, a happy creation, Caroline Helstone, though sometimes remarkably sweet and engaging, is—if we may venture to say so—a failure. . . . Mrs Pryor, in the capital event of her life . . . belies the most indisputable laws of our nature, in becom-ing an unnatural mother,—from some absurd prepossession that her child *must* be bad, wicked, and the cause of anguish to her, because it is pretty! The case is this. She marries a very handsome man, who illtreats her; the fine gentleman turns out a brute. A child is born. This child, which universal experience forces us to exclaim must have been the darling consolation of its miserable mother; this child, over whom the mother would have wept scalding tears in secret, hugging it closer to her bosom to assure her fluttering heart, that in the midst of all her wretchedness, *this* joy remained, that in the midst of all the desolation of home, *this* exquisite comfort was not denied her:—yet this child, we are informed, she parts with, *because* it is pretty! . . . 'A form so straight and fine, I argued, *must* conceal a mind warped and cruel!' Really this is midsummer madness! Before the child had shown whether its beauty *did* conceal perversity, the mother shuts her heart against it! Currer Bell! If under your heart had ever stirred a child, if to your bosom a babe had ever been pressed,—that mysterious part of your being towards which all the rest of it was

drawn, in which your whole soul was transported and absorbed,—
never could you have *imagined* such a falsehood as that! ...

G. H. Lewes, *Edinburgh Review*, vol. XCI, 1850, pp. 153-73.

Villette

... Currer Bell, by hardly *earning* her experience, has, at least, won
her knowledge in a field of action where more can sympathize; though
we cannot speak of sympathy, or of ourselves as in any sense sharing
in it, without a protest against the outrages on decorum, the moral
perversity, the toleration of, nay, indifference to vice which deform
her first powerful picture of a desolate woman's trials and sufferings—
faults which make *Jane Eyre* a dangerous book, and which must leave
a permanent mistrust of the author on all thoughtful and scrupulous
minds. But however alloyed with blame this sympathy has necessarily
been, there are indications of its having cheered her and done her
good. ... In many important moral points *Villette* is an improvement
on its predecessors. The author has gained both in amiability and
propriety since she first presented herself to the world,—soured, coarse,
and grumbling; an alien, it might seem, from society, and amenable
to none of its laws. ...

While we commend the point and graphic power of Currer Bell's
best style, we must explain that many parts of this book do not deserve
this praise. Many passages are turgid, flighty, unreasonable, or otherwise objectionable, and involving subjects not suited for composition
at all. Thus, in the holidays, when left to herself, she has a nervous
fever, and in the course of it has excited thoughts, and does eccentric
things. Such matters are too much like dreams, be they fancy or experience, to be otherwise than irksome to the reader. ...

The moral purpose of this work seems to be to demand for a certain
class of minds a degree of sympathy not hitherto accorded to them; a
class of which Lucy Snowe is the type, who must be supposed to
embody much of the authoress's own feelings and experience, all
going one way to express a character which finds itself unworthily
represented by person and manner, conscious of power, equally and
painfully conscious of certain drawbacks, which throw this superiority
into shade and almost hopeless disadvantage. For such she demands
room to expand, love, tenderness, and a place in happy domestic
life. But in truth she draws a character unfit for this home which she
yearns for. We want a woman at our hearth; and her impersonations
are without the feminine element, infringers of modest restraints,
despisers of bashful fears, self-reliant, contemptuous of prescriptive
decorum; their own unaided reason, their individual opinion of right
and wrong, discreet or imprudent, sole guides of conduct and rules of

manners,—the whole hedge of immemorial scruple and habit broken down and trampled upon. We will sympathize with Lucy Snowe as being fatherless and penniless, and are ready, if this were all, to wish her a husband and a fireside less trying than M. Paul's must be, unless reformed out of all identity; but we cannot offer even the affections of our fancy (the right and due of every legitimate heroine) to her unscrupulous, and self-dependent intellect—to that whole habit of mind which, because it feels no reverence, can never inspire for itself that one important, we may say, indispensable element of man's true love. . . .

Anon, *Christian Remembrancer*, vol. XXV, 1853, pp. 423–43.

. . . It is a work of astonishing power and passion. From its pages there issues an influence of truth as healthful as a mountain breeze. Contempt of conventions in all things, in style, in thought, even in the art of story-telling, here visibly springs from the independent originality of a strong mind nurtured in solitude. As a novel, in the ordinary sense of the word, *Villette* has few claims; as a *book*, it is one which, having read, you will not easily forget. It is quite true that the episode of Miss Marchmont, early in the first volume, is unnecessary, having no obvious connexion with the plot or the characters; but with what wonderful imagination is it painted! Where shall we find such writing as in that description of her last night, wherein the memories of bygone years come trooping in upon her with a vividness partaking of the last energy of life? It is true also that the visit to London is unnecessary, and has many unreal details. Much of the book seems to be brought in merely that the writer may express something which is in her mind; but at any rate she *has* something in her mind and expresses it as no other can. . . .

Let us . . . note the melodramatic character of Madame Beck, who passes into unreality simply from the want of a little light and shade, and the occasional indistinctness in the drawing of John Bretton. Currer Bell has also the fault of running metaphors to death sometimes, and is oppressively fond of the allegorical expression of emotions; thus making passages look mechanical and forced, which if more directly put before us would be very powerful. The power with which she writes at times is marvellous. . . .

Indeed it is as a book that *Villette* most affects us, and every chapter contains or suggests matter for discourse. We say emphatically, a book; meaning by a book, the utterance of an original mind. In this world, as Goethe tells us, 'there are so few voices, and so many echoes;' there are so few books, and so many volumes—so few persons thinking and speaking for themselves, so many reverberating the vague noises of others. Among the few stands *Villette*. In it we read the actual thoughts and feelings of a strong, struggling soul; we hear the cry of pain from one who has loved passionately, and who has sorrowed sorely. Indeed, no more distinct characteristic of Currer Bell's génius can be named, than the depth of her capacity for all passionate emotions. . . .

Indeed, one may say of Currer Bell, what a contemporary has already said, that her genius finds its fittest illustration in her 'Rochesters' and 'Jane Eyres'; they are men and women of deep feeling, clear intellects, vehement tempers, bad manners, ungraceful, yet loveable persons. Their address is *brusque,* perhaps unpleasant, but, at any rate, individual, direct, free from 'shams' and conventions of all kinds. They outrage good taste, yet they fascinate. You dislike them at first, yet you learn to love them. The power that is in them makes its vehement way right to your heart. Propriety, ideal outline, good features, good manners, ordinary thought, ordinary speech, are not to be demanded of them. They are the 'Mirabeaus of Romance'.

If, as critics, we have one thing to say with regard to the future, it is, that Currer Bell, in her next effort, should bestow more pains on her story. With so much passion, with so much power of transmuting experience into forms of enduring fiction, she only needs the vehicle of an interesting story to surpass the popularity of *Jane Eyre.*

G. H. Lewes, *Westminster Review*, New Series vol. III, 1853, pp. 485–91.

DAVID CECIL

Charlotte Brontë

. . . She was a very naïve writer, her faults have the naked crudeness of a child's faults; and in consequence we pass with a sharper jolt from her good passages to her bad. For example, like Dickens', her books are badly constructed. But this does not mean, as it does with him, that the structure is conventional, that the emphasis of the interest falls in a different place from the emphasis of the plot. There is not enough structure in her books to be conventional; their plots are too indeterminate to have an emphasis. Her books . . . are, but for the continued presence of certain figures, incoherent. Nor is this because they are like *Pickwick*, a succession of adventures only connected by a hero. No, each is a drama: but not one drama. Charlotte Brontë will embark on a dramatic action and then, when it is half finished, without warning abandon it for another, equally dramatic, but without bearing on what has come before or will follow after. The first quarter of *Jane Eyre* is about Jane's life as a child; the next half is devoted to her relation with Rochester: in the last quarter of the book, St John Rivers appears, and the rest of the book, except for the final chapters, is concerned with her relation to him. However, *Jane Eyre* does maintain a continuous interest in one central figure. *Villette* and *Shirley* do not even possess this frail principle of unity. The first three chapters of *Villette* are concerned wholly with the child Polly; Lucy Snowe is merely a narrator. In Chapter Four she suddenly takes the centre of the stage; but only to follow the same capricious career as Jane Eyre. After a brief interlude describing her association with Miss Marchmont, she is whisked off to the continent, where for several hundred pages the book is wholly concerned in describing her dawning intimacy with Dr John. But just when this seems likely to reach a culmination the centre of the interest again changes. Poor Dr John is cavalierly dismissed to the position of a minor figure: and his place is taken by Paul Emanuel. In *Shirley* Charlotte Brontë does attempt a more regular scheme. But the result of her effort is only to show her disastrous inability to sustain it. Not only is the story cumbered up with a number of minor characters like the Yorke family and Mrs Pryor, who have no contribution to make to the main action; but that action is itself split into two independent parts. The first centres round Caroline, the second round Shirley; nor has the book any continuous theme of interest in relation to which the two parts combine to form a single whole. Once fully launched on her surging flood of self-revelation, Charlotte Brontë is far above pausing to attend to so paltry a consideration as artistic unity.

She does not pause to consider probability either. Charlotte Brontë's incapacity to make a book coherent as a whole is only equalled by her incapacity to construct a plausible machinery of action for its component parts. Her plots are not dull; but they have every other defect that a plot could have; they are at once conventional, confusing and unlikely.... The stories of her masterpieces, *Jane Eyre* and *Villette*, are, if regarded in a rational aspect, unbelievable from start to finish. *Jane Eyre*, and here too Charlotte Brontë shows herself like Dickens, is a roaring melodrama. But the melodrama of *Bleak House* itself seems sober compared with that of *Jane Eyre*. Not one of the main incidents on which its action turns but is incredible. It is incredible that Rochester should hide a mad wife on the top floor of Thornfield Hall, and hide her so imperfectly that she constantly gets loose and roams yelling about the house, without any of his numerous servants and guests suspecting anything: it is incredible that Mrs Reed, a conventional if disagreeable woman, should conspire to cheat Jane Eyre out of a fortune because she had been rude to her as a child of ten: it is supremely incredible that when Jane Eyre collapses on an unknown doorstep after her flight from Rochester it should turn out to be the doorstep of her only surviving amiable relations. *Villette* has not a melodramatic plot. But by a majestic feat of literary perversity Charlotte Brontë manages to make this quiet chronicle of a school teacher as bristling with improbability as *Jane Eyre*. She stretches the long arm of coincidence till it becomes positively dislocated. It is possible to believe that the only man who happened to be on the spot to assist Lucy Snowe's arrival in Belgium was her long-lost cousin, Graham Bretton. It is harder to believe that he should again be the only man on the spot to help her when she faints in the street six months later. It is altogether impossible to believe that he and his mother should nurse her through an illness without recognizing her, though she had stayed for months in their house only a few years before; and that finally he should rescue another girl and that she should turn out to be his only other female friend of childhood....

Nor are her faults of form her only faults. Her imagination did not know the meaning of the word restraint. This does not appear so much in her narrative, for there imagination is confined to its proper function of creating atmosphere and suggesting the stress of passion. But now and again she allows herself an interval in which to give it free rein: Caroline has a dream, Jane Eyre is inspired to paint a symbolic picture, Shirley Keeldar indulges in a flight of visionary meditation. And then across the page surges a seething cataract of Gothic romanticism and personification, spectres, demons, bleeding swords, angelic countenances, made noisy with all the ejaculation, reiteration and apostrophe that a turgid rhetoric can supply. Even if such passages were good in themselves they put the rest of the book out of focus—how can Madame Beck or Mr Helstone stand out clear before us if they are befogged by these huge cloudy symbols of a high romance? But they are not good in themselves. They are obscure, pretentious, and at times ridiculous.

For she can be ridiculous. And this brings us to another of her defects—her lack of humour. Not that she is wholly without it. Like all the great Victorian novelists, she has a real and delightful vein of her own. But she does not strike this vein often: and when she does not she shows herself as little humorous as it is possible to be. She often means to be amusing. Every book contains attempts to brighten the prevailing atmosphere of murky passion by a satirical flight, a comic curate, Mr Sweeting, a comic dowager, Baroness Ingram of Ingram Hall. But Charlotte Brontë was about as well-equipped to be a satirist as she was to be a ballet-dancer. Satire demands acute observation and a light touch. Charlotte Brontë, indifferent to the outside world and generally in a state of tension, observes little, and never

speaks lightly of anything. In consequence her satirical darts fall wide
of the mark and as ponderous as lead. . . .

But though her lack of humour prevents her amusing us when
she means to, it often amuses us very much when she does not. Her
crudeness, her lack of restraint, and the extreme seriousness with
which she envisages life, combine to deprive her of any sense of ironic
proportion. What could be more comic, if considered in the clear daylight of commonsense, than the scene in *Villette* where Lucy Snowe
is called upon to play the part of a young man in some amateur theat-
ricals: her horrified determination not to wear male costume, Mlle
Zélie's determination that she shall, and the compromise, a purple
crêpe skirt surmounted by a tail-coat and top-hat, attired in which she
finally appears before the footlights? Not less absurd are the Byronic
wooings of Rochester, dressed up in the shawl and bonnet of an old
gypsy woman. Yet Charlotte Brontë describes both scenes with the
same agitated earnestness with which she describes Mrs Reed's death;
and as a result they seem even more ridiculous than before. Her
dialogue, too, is often preposterous, especially when she leaves that
territory of the heart which is her native country to reproduce the
chit-chat of conventional life. . . .

Even within her territory, even in love-scenes, she has her moments
of bathos. After half-an-hour's ardent wooing, Mr Rochester makes a
formal declaration. 'You, poor and obscure, and small and plain as you
are—I entreat to accept me as a husband.' Louis Moore is more
flowery, but hardly more flattering: 'Sister of the spotted, bright,
quick, fiery leopard . . . I am not afraid of you, my leopardess: I dare
live for you and with you from this hour till my death. Now, then I
have you: you are mine: I will never let you go . . . You are younger,
frailer, feebler and more ignorant than I.' At Charlotte Brontë's most
inspired moments, the reader is often brought up sharp by an involun-
tary splutter of laughter. . . .

Charlotte Brontë fails, and fails often, over the most important part
of a novelist's work—over character. Even at her best she is not
among the greatest drawers of character. Her secondary figures do not
move before us with the solid reality of Jane Austen's: seen as they
are through the narrow lens of her heroines' temperament, it is
impossible that they should. And the heroines themselves are presented too subjectively for us to see them in the round as we see Maggie
Tulliver or Emma Bovary. Nor is her failure solely due to the limitations imposed by her angle of approach. Since she feels rather than
understands, she cannot penetrate to the inner structure of a character
to discover its basic elements. Most of her characters are only presented fragmentarily as they happen to catch the eye of her heroine;
but in the one book, *Shirley*, in which she does try to present them

objectively, they are equally fragmentary. And sometimes they are not only fragmentary, they are lifeless. Her satirical, realistic figures, of course, are especially lifeless. The curates in *Shirley,* the house-party in *Jane Eyre,* these are as garishly unreal as the cardboard puppets in a toy theatre. . . .

Charlotte Brontë felt far too remote from that unaccountable wild animal called man to try to get inside him. On the few occasions when she does try, she makes the same mistake as Mrs Gaskell: Crimsworth and Louis Moore, divested of their bass voices and moustaches, are stormy girls just like the rest of her heroines. But as a rule Charlotte Brontë errs in the other extreme. Ignorant what men are like, but convinced that at any rate they must be unlike women, she endows them only with those characteristics she looks on as particularly male: and accentuates these to such a degree that they cease to be human at all. No flesh-and-blood man could be so exclusively composed of violence and virility and masculine vanity as Mr Rochester. . . . Charlotte Brontë's more orthodox heroes like Dr John have not even got imaginative life; they are mere tedious aggregations of good qualities, painted figureheads of virtue like the heroes of Scott. Only in Paul Emanuel has Charlotte Brontë drawn a hero who is also a living man. And he is deliberately presented on unheroic lines. For more than two-thirds of the story in which he appears, we are unaware that he is meant to be anything but a grotesque 'character part'.

Charlotte Brontë's hand does not only falter over her heroes. In Caroline and Shirley, her two objectively-conceived heroines, it is equally uncertain. Both are departures from her usual type. Caroline is described as gentle, sweet and charming, Shirley as charming, brilliant and high-spirited. In company they sustain their rôles convincingly enough. But the moment they are alone they change, they become like each other and unlike either of the characters in which they first appear: in fact, like Crimsworth and Louis Moore, they reveal themselves as two more portraits of that single woman whose other names are Jane Eyre, Lucy Snowe and Charlotte Brontë.

Formless, improbable, humourless, exaggerated, uncertain in their handling of character—there is assuredly a great deal to be said against Charlotte Brontë's novels. So much, indeed, that one may well wonder if she is a good novelist at all. All the same she is; she is even great. Her books are as living today as those of Dickens; and for the same reason. They have creative imagination; and creative imagination of the most powerful kind, able to assimilate to its purpose the strongest feelings, the most momentous experiences. Nor is it intermittent in its actions. Charlotte Brontë, and here again she is like Dickens, is, even at her worst, imaginative. Miss Ingram herself, though she may be a lifeless dummy, is described by Jane Eyre in tones that are far from lifeless. So that the scenes in which she appears, preposterous though they may be, are not lifeless either. Every page of Charlotte Brontë's novels burns and breathes with vitality. Out of her improbabilities and her absurdities, she constructed an original vision of life; from the scattered, distorted fragments of experience which managed to penetrate her huge self-absorption, she created a world.

But her limitations make it very unlike the life of any other novelist's world. For, unhelped as she is by any great power of observation and analysis, her world is almost exclusively an imaginary world. Its character and energy derive nothing important from the character and energy of the world she purports to describe; they are the character and energy of her own personality. . . .

From the chapter on Charlotte Brontë in *Early Victorian Novelists*, Constable, London, 1934. Penguin Books, 1948, pp. 87–114.

KATHLEEN TILLOTSON

Jane Eyre

For the peculiar unity of *Jane Eyre,* the use of the heroine as narrator is mainly responsible. All is seen from the vantage-ground of the single experience of the central character, with which experience the author has imaginatively identified herself, and invited the engagement, again even to the point of imaginative identification, of every reader. . . .

The single point of view may be easily held at the circumference of the narrative and the emotional interest; but Jane continually, quietly, triumphantly occupies the centre, never receding into the role of mere reflector or observer—as does David Copperfield for several chapters at a time. Nor is she ever seen ironically, with the author hovering just visibly beyond her, hinting at her obtuseness and self-deception; an effect well-contrived, for example, by Dickens, notably in the Steerforth scenes of *David Copperfield*, and almost pervasively in *Great Expectations*; by Mrs Gaskell in *Cousin Phillis*; and by Stevenson in *Kidnapped*. These are masterpieces of first-person narrative, but they all sacrifice something that *Jane Eyre* retains; the ironic hovering sets the reader at a further distance from the central character—invited to understand it better than it does itself, he admires it, and identifies himself with it, a shade the less. But the reader of *Jane Eyre* at best keeps pace with the heroine, with her understanding of events (it

would be a safe assumption that every reader shares her suspicions of
Grace Poole) and of character, including her own. A special difficulty
of presenting a central character in first-person narration (and one
more incident to heroines, since custom allows women less latitude
here) is that of combining enough self-description and self-analysis
to define, with enough self-forgetfulness to attract. This difficulty also
Charlotte Brontë circumvents.... Jane is self-critical, but also self-
respecting; her modesty attracts while never making the reader take
her at her own initial valuation. We watch a personality discovering
itself not by long introspection but by a habit of keeping pace with
her own experience. It is from her own explicit record that we are
convinced both of her plainness and her charm, her delicacy and her
endurance, her humility and her pride. Contrivance is never obtrusive
and on a first reading probably unnoticed as such; in the rapid current
of the narrative the deliberate contribution of others' view of her is
accepted unconsciously as part of our picture of Jane. 'If she were a nice,
pretty child, one might compassionate her forlornness; but one really
cannot care for such a little toad as that.' The speaker (Abbot, the
commonplace heartless servant, deflecting Bessie's first stirrings of
pity) is just enough defined for the testimony to be given due but not
excessive weight. Five chapters and a few weeks later, in the sweep of
Helen Burns's impassioned sermon, comes this, 'I read a sincere
nature in your ardent eyes and on your clear front';[1] again, we know
the witness and can weigh the testimony. At Thornfield, Mr
Rochester's half-irritated speculations on Jane's appearance and nature
build up a still clearer definition; but we are so much occupied in
discovering his own still more mysterious character and attitude that
we hardly notice *how* we are being helped to see Jane.

'Eight years! ... No wonder you have rather the look of another
world. ...'[2]
'By my word! there is something singular about you', said he:
'you have the air of a little nonnette; quaint, quiet, grave, and
simple, as you sit with your hands before you, and your eyes
generally bent on the carpet (except, by-the-by, when they are
directed piercingly to my face; as just now for instance). ...'[3]

Even when, disguised as the gipsy fortune-teller, he describes and
interprets her character at length,[4] the situation justifies it; as the
gipsy's testimony, it is accepted as the oracular revelation of the
true Jane; as Mr Rochester's, it is evidence alike of his love and
understanding, and of the 'finest fibre of [her] nature'; as yet not

[1] Ch. viii.   [2] Ch. xiii.
[3] Ch. xiv.   [4] Ch. xix.

consciously realized by him. All that has gone before and follows in the novel is embedded in his concluding words:

> The forehead declares, 'Reason sits firm and holds the reins, and she will not let the feelings burst away and hurry her to wild chasms. The passions may rage furiously, like true heathens, as they are; and the desires may imagine all sorts of vain things: but judgment shall still have the last word in every argument, and the casting vote in every decision. Strong wind, earthquake shock, and fire may pass by: I shall follow the guiding of that still small voice which interprets the dictates of conscience.'

Their irony is only in his unawareness that this very reason, judgement, and conscience will frustrate him.

Jane keeps no journal and writes no letters; she simply re-enters her experience, and even the vision of herself as retrospective recorder is rare and delicately timed:

> What a consternation of soul was mine that dreary afternoon! How all my brain was in tumult, and all my heart in insurrection! Yet in what darkness, what dense ignorance, was the mental battle fought! I could not answer the ceaseless inward question—*why* I thus suffered; now at a distance of—I will not say how many years, I see it clearly.
> I was a discord in Gateshead-hall: I was like nobody there: I had nothing in harmony with Mrs Reed or her children, or her chosen vassalage. . . .[1]
> I was almost as hard beset by him now as I had been once before, in a different way, by another. I was a fool both times. To have yielded then would have been an error of principle; to have yielded now would have been an error of judgment. So I think at this hour, when I look back to the crisis through the quiet medium of time: I was unconscious of folly at the instant.[2]

Rarely in self-analysis, though more often in description, are we aware of 'the quiet medium of time'; the tense of most of the novel is the just-after-present. . . . Truth to immediate experience extends to minutest detail; the description of Miss Temple is partly retrospective—'round curls, according to the fashion of those times . . . watches were not so common then as now . . .' but it ends with a quiet return to the child's view—'Miss Temple—Maria Temple, as I afterwards saw the name written in a prayer-book entrusted to me to carry to church.'[3]

[1] Ch. ii.   [2] Ch. xxxv.   [3] Ch. v.

The consistency and flexibility of the first person method is unusual, and its use in a narrative of childhood perhaps an absolute novelty in fiction. The novel would have lost incalculably had it started later in Jane's life—say, at her setting out for Thornfield. The early chapters are no mere prologue; they expound a situation, introduce and partly account for a character, and initiate the major themes of the whole novel. Presented as a child, she engages interest, sympathy, and admiration, which is yet kept clear . . . of a too generic compassion. The author who launches hero or heroine early in life can count on a special kind of goodwill in the reader—which is perhaps defined by merely citing the instances of Fanny Price, David Copperfield, Henry Esmond, Pip, Maggie Tulliver, and Molly Gibson. And by representing typical experiences and responses, the author also draws upon everyone's recollections of early consciousness. . . .

But, beyond all other examples in the novel, *Jane Eyre* arrests attention in its opening chapters by disclosing an individual character enmeshed in, yet independent of, unusual circumstances. And it is the opening of a poetic novel; season, scene, and character are interpenetrated:

> There was no possibility of taking a walk that day. We had been wandering, indeed, in the leafless shrubbery an hour in the morning; but since dinner (Mrs Reed, when there was no company, dined early) the cold winter wind had brought with it clouds so sombre, and a rain so penetrating, that further out-door exercise was now out of the question. . . .
> . . . At intervals, while turning over the leaves of my book, I studied the aspect of that winter afternoon. Afar it offered a pale blank of mist and cloud; near, a scene of wet lawn and storm-beat shrub, with ceaseless rain sweeping away wildly before a long and lamentable blast.

It is November—a season which is to recur nine years later in the novel just when the last particulars of Jane's early history are disclosed.[1]

An indoor scene on a winter's day; a child in disgrace, excluded from the family circle, reading a book in a curtained window-seat; a creature dependent, captive, yet with the liberty of adventure in imagination—a window to look out of, a book to read and pictures on which to build fancies. The double impression of constraint and freedom is burnt into the mind in those first few paragraphs; it is accompanied by the symbol (to become recurrent) of the window. From this retreat we see her dragged out, bullied, insulted; she is a terrified

---

[1] Chs. xxxii-xxxiii; the date, 5 November, is specified.

cornered animal—but one that fights back, with intellectual and imaginative resourcefulness.

> The cut bled, the pain was sharp: my terror had passed its climax; other feelings succeeded.
> 'Wicked and cruel boy!' I said. 'You are like a murderer—you are like a slave-driver—you are like the Roman emperors!'
> I had read Goldsmith's History of Rome, and had formed my opinion of Nero, Caligula, etc. Also I had drawn parallels in silence, which I never thought thus to have declared aloud.

John Reed's taunts skilfully conceal a piece of formal exposition, in which the outline of Jane's situation is conveyed to us—a child without status or adult protector. Not until the second chapter is her actual relation to the Reed family stated, and the details of her origin wait until the third, where she overhears the servants' gossip. Meanwhile the terrors of imagination increase the agony of her imprisonment in the Red Room. But yet the tone is kept low, with no overt bid for pity; her captors are not monsters, their point of view is a valid one ('I was a discord in Gateshead-hall'); Bessie pities her for a moment, before roast onion supervenes; and the large gestures of romance are explicitly avoided:

> No severe or prolonged bodily illness followed this incident of the red-room. . . .
> 'No; I should not like to belong to poor people. . . .' I was not heroic enough to purchase liberty at the price of caste.[1] . . .

Another opportunity for heightening is balked in the interests of deeper truthfulness at the child's verbal triumph over Mrs Reed:

> I was left there alone—winner of the field. It was the hardest battle I had fought, and the first victory I had gained. . . . First, I smiled to myself and felt elate; but this fierce pleasure subsided in me as fast as did the accelerated throb of my pulses. A child cannot quarrel with its elders as I had done; cannot give its furious feelings uncontrolled play as I had given mine; without experiencing afterwards the pang of remorse and the chill of reaction.[2]

And this sense of the victory of impulse turning to ashes is a part of the novel's theme.

The deliberate dryness of tone and accompanying self-criticism make the early chapters less harrowing than they could have been— and than the Murdstone chapters of *David Copperfield* are. The facts

[1] Ch. iii.   [2] Ch. iv.

are terrible enough; how terrible is quietly indicated at the appearance
of the apothecary Mr Lloyd as she revives from her fainting fit:

> I felt an inexpressible relief, a soothing conviction of protection
> and security, when I knew that there was a stranger in the room;
> an individual not belonging to Gateshead, and not related to
> Mrs Reed.[1]

But they are counterbalanced by our sense of a character growing
from its own inward strength, like grass pushing up between stones.
This growth is reflected in the clear shallow pool of Bessie's

> 'You little sharp thing! you've got quite a new way of talking.
> What makes you so venturesome and hardy?'[2]

The impact of Mr Brocklehurst is the more terrifying from the precise
use of the physical child's-eye view ('I looked up at a black pillar');
but under moral and theological bullying the animal again fights
back:

> 'And what is hell? Can you tell me that?'
> 'A pit full of fire.'
> 'And should you like to fall into that pit and to be burning there
> for ever?'
> 'No, sir.'
> 'What must you do to avoid it?'
> I deliberated a moment; my answer, when it did come, was
> objectionable: 'I must keep in good health, and not die.' . . .
> 'And the Psalms? I hope you like them.'
> 'No, sir.'[3]

The colloquy has more than one echo; the less obvious is the more
valuable in revealing part of the novel's pattern:

> 'But,' was slowly, distinctly read, 'the fearful, the unbelieving, etc.
> shall have their part in the lake which burneth with fire and brim-
> stone, which is the second death.'
> Henceforward, I knew what fate St John feared for me.

> 'You examine me Miss Eyre; do you think me handsome?'
> 'No, sir.'[5]

The savagery and reserve, sensitiveness and sharp-wittedness that
we are to know in Jane at eighteen are hers at ten. 'Never was anything
at once so frail and so indomitable. . . .'[6]
Above all, in these early chapters there is gradually disengaged
from the generic impression of a child robbed of its birthright the

---

[1] Ch. iii.   [2] Ch. iv.   [3] Ch. iv.
[4] Ch. xxxv.   [5] Ch. xiv.   [6] xxvii

individual figure of a heart hungering for affection. Save for a few unconsciously dropped crumbs from Bessie, at Gateshead her bread is stones; in the choric words of Bessie's song 'Men are hard-hearted', and the assurance that 'Kind angels only Watch o'er the steps of the poor orphan child' is as yet barren of comfort; there are no angels in Mr Brocklehurst's religion. Lowood opens inauspiciously, with still harsher physical discomfort—not merely piercingly actual (the taste of the burnt porridge, the starved arms wrapped in pinafores) but symbolic of a loveless order of things.[1] In Helen Burns and Miss Temple appear the first shadowings of hope; the warm fire and the cake from the cupboard in Miss Temple's room are assertions of individual loving-kindness, though also of its limited power; and Helen's comfort in injustice reaches her as from another world:

> ... She chafed my fingers gently to warm them, and went on:—
> 'If all the world hated you, and believed you wicked, while your own conscience approved you, and absolved you from guilt, you would not be without friends.'
> 'No; I know I should think well of myself; but that is not enough: if others don't love me, I would rather die than live—I cannot bear to be solitary and hated, Helen. . . .'[2]

Helen's religious assurances bring calm—but with 'an alloy of inexpressible sadness'. For she has spoken as one facing towards death; and she dies, her message of endurance and trust . . . only half accepted; at her deathbed Jane asks 'Where is God? What is God?'

The vehement, impulsive hunger of her nature is not satisfied at Lowood; it is only assuaged. Summing up eight years of Miss Temple's influence, she says:

> I had imbibed from her something of her nature and much of her habits: more harmonious thoughts; what seemed better regulated feelings had become the inmates of my mind. I had given an allegiance to duty and order; I was quiet; I believed I was content: to the eyes of others, usually even to my own, I appeared a disciplined and subdued character. . . .[3]
> For liberty I gasped; for liberty I uttered a prayer; it seemed scattered on the wind then faintly blowing. . . .

Or if not liberty, 'at least a new servitude'.[4]

From the chapter on *Jane Eyre* in *Novels of the Eighteen Forties*,
Clarendon Press, Oxford, 1954, pp. 257–313.

[1] Ch. xxxiv.   [2] Ch. viii.   [3] Ch. x.
[4] Ch. x.

ROBERT B. HEILMAN

Charlotte Brontë's New Gothic

... Charlotte's story is conventional; formally she is for 'reason' and 'real life'; but her characters keep escaping to glorify 'feeling' and 'Imagination'. Feeling is there in the story—evading repression, in author or in character; ranging from nervous excitement to emotional absorption; often tense and peremptory; sexuality, hate, irrational impulse, grasped, given life, not merely named and pigeonholed. This is Charlotte's version of Gothic: in her later novels an extraordinary thing. In that incredibly eccentric history, *The Gothic Quest*, Montague Summers asserts that the 'Gothic novel of sensibility ... draws its emotionalism and psychology ... from the work of Samuel Richardson.' When this line of descent continues in the Brontës, the vital feeling moves toward an intensity, a freedom, and even an abandon virtually non-existent in historical Gothic and rarely approached in Richardson. From Angria on, Charlotte's women vibrate with passions that the fictional conventions only partly constrict or gloss over—in the centre an almost violent devotedness that has in it at once a fire of independence, a spiritual energy, a vivid sexual responsiveness, and, along with this, self-righteousness, a sense of power, sometimes self-pity and envious competitiveness. To an extent the heroines are 'unheroined,' unsweetened. Into them there has come a new sense of the dark side of feeling and personality....

From childhood terrors to all those mysteriously threatening sights, sounds, and injurious acts that reveal the presence of some malevolent force and that anticipate the holocaust at Thornfield, the traditional Gothic in *Jane Eyre* has often been noted, and as often disparaged. It need not be argued that Charlotte Brontë did not reach the heights while using hand-me-down devices, though a tendency to work through the conventions of fictional art was a strong element in her make-up. This is true of all her novels, but it is no more true than her countertendency to modify, most interestingly, these conventions. In both *Villette* and *Jane Eyre* Gothic is used but characteristically is undercut.

Jane Eyre hears a 'tragic ... preternatural ... laugh', but this is at 'high noon' and there is 'no circumstance of ghostliness'; Grace Poole, the supposed laugher, is a plain person, than whom no 'apparition less romantic or less ghostly could ... be conceived'; Charlotte apologizes ironically to the 'romantic reader' for telling 'the plain

truth' that Grace generally bears a 'pot of porter'. Charlotte almost
habitually revises 'old Gothic', the relatively crude mechanisms of
fear, with an infusion of the anti-Gothic. When Mrs Rochester first
tried to destroy Rochester by fire, Jane 'baptized' Rochester's bed and
heard Rochester 'fulminating strange anathemas at finding himself
lying in a pool of water'. The introduction of comedy as a palliative
of straight Gothic occurs on a large scale when almost seventy-five
pages are given to the visit of the Ingram-Eshton party to mysterious
Thornfield; here Charlotte, as often in her novels, falls into the
manner of the Jane Austen whom she despised. When Mrs Rochester
breaks loose again and attacks Mason, the presence of guests lets
Charlotte play the nocturnal alarum for at least a touch of comedy:
Rochester orders the frantic women not to 'pull me down or strangle
me'; and 'the two dowagers, in vast white wrappers, were bearing down
on him like ships in full sail'.

The symbolic also modifies the Gothic, for it demands of the
reader a more mature and complicated response than the relatively
simple thrill or momentary intensity of feeling sought by primitive
Gothic. When mad Mrs Rochester, seen only as 'the foul German
spectre—the Vampyre', spreads terror at night, that is one thing; when,
with the malicious insight that is the paradox of her madness, she
tears the wedding veil in two and thus symbolically destroys the
planned marriage, that is another thing, far less elementary as art.
The midnight blaze that ruins Thornfield becomes more than a
shock when it is seen also as the fire of purgation; the grim, almost
roadless forest surrounding Ferndean is more than a harrowing
stage-set when it is also felt as a symbol of Rochester's closed-in life.

The point is that in various ways Charlotte manages to make the
patently Gothic more than a stereotype. But more important is that
she instinctively finds new ways to achieve the ends served by old
Gothic—the discovery and release of new patterns of feeling, the
intensification of feeling. Though only partly unconventional, Jane is
nevertheless so portrayed as to evoke new feelings rather than merely
exercise old ones. As a girl she is lonely, 'passionate', 'strange', 'like
nobody there'; she feels superior, rejects poverty, talks back precoc-
iously, tells truths bluntly, enjoys 'the strangest sense of freedom',
tastes 'vengeance'; she experiences a nervous shock which is said to
have a lifelong effect, and the doctor says 'nerves not in a good
state'; she can be 'reckless and feverish', 'bitter and truculent'; at
Thornfield she is restless, given to 'bright visions', letting 'imagination'
picture an existence full of 'life, fire, feeling'. Thus Charlotte leads
away from standardized characterization towards new levels of human
reality, and hence from stock responses towards a new kind of passionate
engagement.

Charlotte moves towards depth in various ways that have an immed-iate impact like that of Gothic. Jane's strange, fearful, symbolic dreams are not mere thrillers but reflect the tensions of the engagement period, the stress of the wedding-day debate with Rochester, and the longing for Rochester after she has left him. The final Thornfield dream, with its vivid image of a hand coming through a cloud in place of the expected moon, is in the surrealistic vein that appears most sharply in the extraordinary pictures that Jane draws at Thornfield: here Charlotte is plumbing the psyche, not inventing a weird *décor*. Like-wise in the telepathy scene, which Charlotte, unlike Defoe in dealing with a similar episode, does her utmost to actualize: 'The feeling was not like an electric shock; but it was quite as sharp, as strange, as startling: ... that inward sensation ... with all its unspeakable strangeness ... like an inspiration ... wondrous shock of feeling. ...' In her flair for the surreal, in her plunging into feeling that is without status in the ordinary world of the novel, Charlotte discovers a new dimension of Gothic.

She does this most thoroughly in her portrayal of characters and of the relations between them. If in Rochester we see only an Angrian-Byronic hero and a Charlotte wish-fulfilment figure (the two identi-fications which to some readers seem entirely to place him), we miss what is more significant, the exploration of personality that opens up new areas of feeling in intersexual relationships. Beyond the 'grim', the 'harsh', the eccentric, the almost histrionically cynical that super-ficially distinguish Rochester from conventional heroes, there is some-thing almost Lawrentian: Rochester is 'neither tall nor graceful'; his eyes can be 'dark, irate, and piercing'; his strong features 'took my feelings from my own power and fettered them in his'. Without using the vocabulary common to us, Charlotte is presenting maleness and physicality, to which Jane responds directly. She is 'assimilated' to him by 'something in my brain and my heart, in my blood and nerves'; she 'must love' and 'could not unlove' him; the thought of parting from him is 'agony'. Rochester's oblique amatory manoeuvres become almost punitive in the Walter-to-Griselda style and once reduce her to sobbing 'convulsively'; at times the love-game borders on a power-game. Jane, who prefers 'rudeness' to 'flattery', is an instinctive evoker of passion: she learns 'the pleasure of vexing and soothing him by turns' and pursues a 'system' of working him up 'to considerable irritation' and coolly leaving him; when, as a result, his caresses become grimaces, pinches, and tweaks, she records that, sometimes at least, she 'decidedly preferred these fierce favours'. She reports, 'I crushed his hand ... red with the passionate pressure'; she 'could not ... see God for his creature', and in her devotion Rochester senses 'an earnest, religious energy'.

Charlotte's remoulding of stock feeling reaches a height when she sympathetically portrays Rochester's efforts to make Jane his mistress; here the stereotyped seducer becomes a kind of lost nobleman of passion, and of specifically physical passion: 'Every atom of your flesh is as dear to me as my own....' The intensity of the pressure which he puts upon her is matched, not by the fear and revulsion of the popular heroine, but by a responsiveness which she barely masters: 'The crisis was perilous; but not without its charm...' She is 'tortured by a sense of remorse at thus hurting his feelings'; at the moment of decision 'a hand of fiery iron grasped my vitals... blackness, burning! ... my intolerable duty'; she leaves in 'despair'; and after she has left, 'I longed to be his; I panted to return...'—and for the victory of principle 'I abhorred myself... I was hateful in my own eyes', This extraordinary openness to feeling, this escape from the bondage of the trite, continues in the Rivers relationship, which is a structural parallel to the Rochester affair: as in Rochester the old sex villain is seen in a new perspective, so in Rivers the clerical hero is radically refashioned; and Jane's almost accepting a would-be husband is given the aesthetic status of a regrettable yielding to a seducer. Without a remarkable liberation from conventional feeling Charlotte could not fathom the complexity of Rivers—the earnest and dutiful clergyman distraught by a profound inner turmoil of conflicting 'drives': sexuality, restlessness, hardness, pride, ambition ('fever in his vitals', 'inexorable as death'); the hypnotic, almost inhuman potency of his influence on Jane, who feels 'a freezing spell', 'an awful charm', an 'iron shroud'; the relentlessness, almost the unscrupulousness, of his wooing, the resultant fierce struggle (like that with Rochester), Jane's brilliantly perceptive accusation, '... you almost hate me ... you would kill me. You are killing me now'; and yet her mysterious near-surrender: 'I was tempted to cease struggling with him—to rush down the torrent of his will into the gulf of his existence, and there lose my own.'

Aside from partial sterilization of banal Gothic by dry factuality and humour, Charlotte goes on to make a much more important—indeed, a radical—revision of the mode: in *Jane Eyre* and in the other novels ... that discovery of passion, that rehabilitation of the extra-rational, which is the historical office of Gothic, is no longer oriented in marvellous circumstance but moves deeply into the lesser known realities of human life. This change I describe as the change from 'old Gothic' to 'new Gothic'. The kind of appeal is the same; the fictional method is utterly different. ...

From 'Charlotte Brontë's New Gothic' in *From Jane Austen to Joseph Conrad*, Ed. Robert C. Rathburn and Martin Steinmann Jr., University of Minnesota Press, Minneapolis, 1958, pp. 118-132.

MELVIN R. WATSON

Shirley

... Potentially, *Shirley* (1849) is a better novel than *Jane Eyre*. Set in the early part of the century, played out against the background of international events which affected the economic state of the country, and introducing a serious phase of the Industrial Revolution, *Shirley* has characters and a plot that are often more convincing than the melodramatics of Thornfield Hall and the Byronism of Edward Rochester. Caroline Helstone is in many ways the most attractive of Charlotte Brontë's heroines and many of the minor characters, taken on their own terms, are genuinely interesting. Several scenes at the mill, such as those in Chapters VIII and XIX, arising from Robert Moore's determination to introduce machinery in the weaving industry of the West Riding of Yorkshire, show real dramatic power. Yet it is generally recognized that *Shirley* is actually the weakest of the works which Charlotte herself published, not only because there are false notes and improbable contrivances—these exist in all Brontë fiction—but because the novel never comes together, because insufficient order has been imposed upon the unusually disparate materials.

Perhaps the first and most basic difficulty is with the theme. In Chapter I two big themes are suggested: the religious issue of Dissent versus Establishment and the socio-economic one of frame-breaking. Later we become involved in the personal stories of Caroline Helstone and Shirley Keeldar. The first of these themes is never developed, though it is used occasionally, as when in Chapter VIII, the leader of the frame-breakers turns out to be Moses Barraclough, a Methodist ranter, and when in Chapter XVII the parade for the school feast meets a parade of Dissenters, who are forced to give way. The other three themes make up the body of the book and are connected in various ways, notably through the character of Robert Moore, but they are never successfully blended, largely, I suspect, because Moore is such an unsatisfactory hero. As a manufacturer and businessman, despite his attitude towards the workingman, the reader can understand and even perhaps sympathize with him; but his relationship with the two women can only alienate the reader. Perhaps the trouble is that Charlotte Brontë tried to unite in one person the hard-headed but weakly financed businessman and the romantic lover. No such problem faced her in *Jane Eyre*.

But what about the heroine (or heroines)? The reader is forced to ask the fundamental question, who is the heroine? And the answer is not easy. From the title one would naturally assume it to be Shirley Keeldar, but she is not even introduced until Chapter XI and thereafter there are periods when she is on the sidelines. Her personal story (for the assumed romance between her and Robert Moore turns out to be a red herring) is developed only in the last ten chapters or so, beginning with Chapter XXVI, when Louis Moore, introduced as late as Chapter XXIII after one earlier mention, becomes a main character and her uncle's attempts to marry her off become a matter of some importance. Despite the implicit contradiction of the title and the split in the reader's interest, Caroline would seem to be intended for the heroine. From the time she is introduced in Chapter V she is seldom absent from the stage (and usually her position is near centre) until the latter part when Shirley's love life is developed. But more important, wherever possible the story is told from her point of view. She is the only character whose actions and feelings are analysed, whom we get inside of.

This last characteristic accounts for a good part of the artificiality of the technique. In *Jane Eyre* the first-person point of view had been used consistently and successfully, but in *Shirley,* Charlotte Brontë tried a combination of the omniscient author, which parts of her material required, and the personal point of view. The two are not convincingly blended. Too often one feels that the author is taking unfair advantage of the reader just to maintain suspense. The most obvious example is the handling of Mrs Pryor. Only if the story were told completely from Caroline's point of view, could the secrecy of her identity until the sentimental moment in Chapter XXIV when she gives Caroline something to live for by giving her a mother be justified. It is striking too that the assumed romance between Shirley and Robert Moore is revealed principally through Caroline's sensibilities and the true romance of Shirley and Louis Moore comes to us largely through Caroline's awareness. The fact seems to be that whenever it suits the writer's convenience or the requirements of the plot, material is presented from Caroline's point of view. Otherwise the impersonal technique is used. The way of telling the story in *Jane Eyre* is surer.

In some ways *Shirley* is a richer novel than *Jane Eyre*. There is more variety of plot and character; yet once again this variety is as much a flaw as a virtue, for some of the material seems not to be used functionally in the novel. Take, for example, the curates, who are introduced with much noise in Chapter I and are carefully disposed of in the last chapter: Donne, Malone, and Sweeting run in and out of the story and Malone even takes some part in the action centred in the mill, but they are really lagniappe. The same may be said of Mrs Sykes and her three daughters, who do little more than provide part of the crowd at several of the gatherings. Mr Yorke and his family do at times participate importantly in the action, but the family is principally presented as a group of eccentrics and nothing much is made of the antagonism suggested between Mr Yorke and the Reverend Mr Helstone. If this were a novel of manners, there would be more justification for introducing 'characters', primarily to fill in the canvas; but since there is no evidence that *Shirley* was intended as a picture of society, these elements provide just one more bit of incompletely assimilated material. The truth is that it would have taken more careful craftsmanship than presumably Charlotte Brontë was capable of to whip all these themes and characters and materials into shape. . . .

> From 'Form and Substance in The Brontë Novels', in *From Jane Austen to Joseph Conrad*, Ed. Robert C. Rathburn and Martin Steinmann Jr., University of Minnesota Press, Minneapolis, 1958, pp. 106–117.

ROBERT A. COLBY

Villette and the Life of the Mind

'Miss Brontë has written a hideous, undelightful, convulsed, constricted novel . . . one of the most utterly disagreeable books I ever read.' wrote Matthew Arnold to his friend Arthur Hugh Clough, shortly after the first publication of *Villette*.[1] The novel struck Arnold mainly as a case of morbid religiosity. Only a month later another critic, George Henry Lewes, writing more from the point of view of the amateur psychologist, said of the very same novel: 'It is a work of astonishing power and passion. From its pages there issues an influence of truth as healthful as a mountain breeze.'[2] These are typical of the antithetical responses that *Villette* has always evoked. . . .

By comparison with the steady excitement of *Jane Eyre*, *Villette* may seem to some readers loosely woven and desultory in pace, not so carefully plotted. . . . The romance around which *Villette* principally turns is between two outwardly rather unattractive people, and

---

[1] 21 March 1853, *Letters to Arthur Hugh Clough*, ed. Howard Lowry, O.U.P., London, Vol. I, p.132.
[2] '*Ruth* and *Villette*', *Westminster Review*, Vol. LIX, April 1853, p.485.

nothing much (practically speaking) comes of it. Yet it may still be argued that in many ways Miss Brontë's last novel was her most profound accomplishment. . . .

Villette is most fruitfully approached as Charlotte Brontë's literary, not her literal, autobiography. Lucy Snowe's turbulent emotional experiences may be taken as an analogue of Charlotte Brontë's creative life, in that her achievement of mastery over her morbidly introverted imagination parallels Miss Brontë's own emancipation from the dream world she had envisaged in the Angrian legends of her youth. . . . While throughout the novel passion and rationality, art and nature, romance and reality continuously exert their rival claims on Lucy's imagination, in the end these tensions are resolved. Greater richness is produced also by the contrast between the tragedy of Lucy Snowe and the happier fates of the lesser heroines Polly Home and Ginevra Fanshawe.

Many readers may feel that of the three stories developed in *Villette*, the only one that is really 'done', as Henry James might have put it, is the romance between Lucy Snowe and Monsieur Paul. Had Miss Brontë succeeded in penetrating the other two romances with equal insight perhaps she would have produced a masterpiece on the order and scale of, say, *Middlemarch,* instead of the erratic and uneven masterpiece that *Villette* admittedly is. However, the superficial treatment of the secondary characters actually serves a purpose in the scheme of the novel. Ginevra Fanshawe, who flits over the surface of life, and Polly Home de Bassompierre, who is sheltered from its troubles and vicissitudes, really set off Lucy Snowe, who becomes the most deeply and intensely *engagé* of the three. Lucy is intended to represent a fuller and completer woman—and to pay the price for this plenitude. If one is to feel deeply and live profoundly, one must be prepared also to suffer grandly, we are led to infer.

The characters are contrasted not only by their sensibilities. Significant differences in the descriptions of the three pairs of lovers indicate something also of the Brontëan scale of values with respect to nature and art. Ginevra Fanshawe and her suitor Colonel de Hamal are conceived almost entirely as pseudo art objects. Coquettish Ginevra is likened to 'kitsch' with her blonde curls, rouge, spangles, and sashes, her narcissistic gazing at gaudy polished mirrors, while exuding otto of roses. De Hamal, for his part, is the merry model of the beau and dandy, 'so nicely curled, so booted and gloved and cravated', with his 'low Grecian brow and exquisite classic headpiece'. At one point Polly and Ginevra are contrasted as works of art, Polly being recognized as the more genuine article, 'nature having traced all these details slightly and with a careless hand, in Miss Fanshawe's case, and in Miss de Bassompierre's wrought them to a high and delicate finish'. Frequently both Polly and her suitor Dr John Bretton are made to represent *nature cultivated by art*. Dr John's features 'though well cut, they were not so chiselled, so frittered away, as to lose in power and significance what they gained in unmeaning symmetry'. As for Polly, Lucy affirms, 'I, who had known her as a child, knew or guessed by what a good and strong root her graces held to the firm soil of reality'. Both Polly and Dr John are something between nature and art, creatures perpetually basking in light, like sheltered greenhouse plants. Not so the 'fiery and rash' Lucy Snowe, or Monsieur Paul, with his fierceness of aspect, his 'blueness and fire of glance', his 'strength of sturdy independence in the stringing of his sinews'. Lucy in her plainness and Paul in his outward ugliness are the least aesthetically appealing of the characters of the novel, but by the same token the ones closest to *rude nature*, with her fierce energies and her unpredictable changes. They encompass light and darkness, calm and storm. Their destinies therefore are poetically suitable—Paul perishing and Lucy lamenting amidst the turbulence of nature's elements.

This subtle interpenetration of nature and art really informs the entire novel, binding together the loosely woven first two-thirds of the story with the more taut and tense latter portion. A good part of *Villette*, particularly its early sections, is taken up with literature and the other arts, both explicitly and by allusion. In this novel, on the whole, the arts are associated with passivity and escapism, nature with the active mind and reality. For Lucy, therefore, the arts tend to recede in importance as she becomes less a spectator of and more a direct participant in life. This shift is bound up with the gradual process of self-discovery that Lucy experiences, involving changes of attitude, revisions of judgment, a general re-orientation of her emotions and mind.

Very early in the novel, at the close of the idyllic Bretton episodes, Lucy, gazing down at Little Polly as she sleeps, meditates thus: 'A very unique child . . . How will she bear the shocks and repulses, the humiliations and desolations, which books and my own reason tell me are prepared for all flesh?' This episode, as well as the focal position that the child Polly occupies in general in the Bretton scenes, has led May Sinclair to infer that Miss Brontë at this point really intended Polly to be the heroine of the novel, but that Lucy gradually usurped Polly's role as her creator became more and more absorbed in her romance with Monsieur Paul.[1] Miss Sinclair has missed the point, for what actually happens is that *Lucy becomes a heroine in spite of herself*, discovering that life holds in store for her the grand

[1] Introduction to Everyman edition of *Villette*, London, 1909.

desolation that she thought awaited Polly. Though the tormented Little Polly is hardly mother to the placid Paulina de Bassompierre ... this change is only one of the strange shifts that life reveals to Lucy. So too does she find the crochety old cripple Miss Marchmont a woman of surprising courage and mental resources; the vain flibbertigibbet Ginevra Fanshawe not a 'bad sort' after all; and above all she discovers her deepest love at a source where she would least have suspected it—Monsieur Paul Emanuel.

'Books and my own reason,' as Lucy observes, are at this point her sole source of knowledge about life and people. What she lacks is experience of reality, and that her ensuing adventures provide her. When she is not recalling an actual scene, we can observe in many places Lucy's predisposition to daydream or to think of life in terms of literature. 'I seemed to hold two lives,' Lucy says of herself shortly after her arrival in Villette, 'the life of thought, and that of reality; and provided the former was nourished with a sufficiency of the strange, necromantic joys of fancy, the privileges of the latter might remain limited to daily bread, hourly work, and a roof of shelter.' As her story progresses, Lucy learns to bring these dissociated halves of her life into some kind of fusion. But for much of it fancy takes over. Her frequent references to Christian and Hopeful, Apollyon and the Hill of Despair indicate one book that has nourished her imagination. The Bible is another. (Of Madame Beck: 'Not the agony in Gethsemane, not the death on Calvary could have rung from her eyes one tear.') But she is also deeply immersed in classical myth....

As it happens, life shocks Lucy Snowe out of her reveries, necromantic fancies, and illusions....

Lucy's tendency, when left to her own devices, is to live life vicariously—through other people's lives, or through literature, art, and the theatre. In the Bretton episodes she looks on at the budding puppy romance of Polly and John Graham Bretton as though it were a scene in a play; at the Pension she is forced by Monsieur Paul to act a part in a love drama performed at the school; in the performance of Vashti (really Mme Rachel) which she witnesses with Dr John (Graham Bretton grown up), she sees unleashed on the stage that turbulent emotionalism that she herself represses. Throughout the novel she glides through various fetes and balls, a spectator of the dance of life. The art gallery too offers Lucy substitute experience: the voluptuous 'Cleopatra' in the manner of Peter Paul Rubens is, like Vashti, an objective correlative for the abundant life as yet denied her, and as such is in marked contrast to the genteel set of panels depicting the four ages of woman, from virgin to widow, that Monsieur Paul prefers her to look at....

Before Lucy herself experiences a love tragedy she learns of blighted

romance from others: from Miss Marchmont, whose story sounds
very much like a tale from some keepsake album; then from Monsieur
Paul, who has also suffered the untimely death of a loved one. There is
also the supposed ghost of the nun, a vestige from a Gothic romance,
whom both Lucy and Paul fancy may be the soul of another who was
denied love. In the leisurely paced early portions of the novel, then,
Lucy is mainly an 'outsider' and a passive observer of life lived mainly
by indirection. The novel grows tighter and more tense as she
becomes involved with life more directly....

Contrasted with the episodes of *Villette* that take place indoors—
in lecture halls, concert halls, theatres, art galleries, and ball rooms—
are several, particularly towards the end, that take place in woods
and gardens. Art is thereby posed against Nature, and it is significantly
in a natural environment that Lucy's love for Monsieur Paul blossoms.
The tales she hears him recite in 'les bois et les petits sentiers' sound
Wordsworthian with 'a diction simple in its strength and strong in its
simplicity'. What Lucy obviously means to stress about these tales is
their freedom from artifice, that is, their *un*-literary character. As she
informs us: 'M. Emanuel was not a man to write books ... *His mind
was indeed my library*, and whenever it was opened to me, I entered
bliss.' In one of his tales, we are told, he 'tinted a twilight scene', and
'*Such a picture I have never looked on from artist's pencil*' (Italics
mine). What impresses Lucy about Monsieur Paul, on the whole, is the
intuitiveness of his grasp of experience. We are to understand that
he leads her from literature and art into nature, from vicarious
experience into direct experience, from imitations of life into life
itself....

Lucy's narrative is reminiscence, setting her turbulent feelings and
deep joys and sorrows of the past at a distance that transforms them
to 'emotion recollected in tranquility'. This is the sign of her reconciliation of passion and calm of mind. Memory is her catharsis. Moreover,
in the very framework of *Villette* and in the point of view from
which it is told, there is embedded that circularity of life and literature, romance and reality that envelops its incidents, characters, and
thought. 'I used to think what a delight it would be for one who
loved him better than he loved himself to gather and store up those
handfuls of gold dust, so recklessly flung to heaven's reckless winds,'
Lucy recalls in connection with one of the sylvan story hours. So she
writes a book about a man who didn't write books. *Villette* then is
one of those special novels that we have become more used to in our
century which have a novelist writing a novel at their centre.
Lucy is really observing herself in the process of composing, creating
characters and re-creating herself, and one understands therefore why

she is so preoccupied with the workings of the mind and the imagination.

In this respect *Villette* can be contrasted with *Jane Eyre*. Where Lucy's impulse is to take up the pen, Jane's is to reach for the crayon. Jane feels that she has 'pinned down' a character when she has managed to sketch his lineaments at the drawing board. Lucy, on the other hand, is every minute the writer . . . . As a writer, Lucy is intent upon probing to the *inside* of character, and character *analysis* therefore seems to her more important than mere character *reading*. . . .

Miss Marchmont, the bed-ridden cripple, is the complete reverse of Lucy's colleagues at the school in that she reveals an inner strength belied by a weak exterior. 'She gave me the originality of her character to study,' declares Lucy, 'the steadiness of her virtues . . . the power of her passions, to admire; the truth of her feelings to trust, and for these things I clung to her.' In her brief appearance Miss Marchmont suggests what Lucy is to become: 'A vein of *reason* ever ran through her *passion*; she was *logical* even when *fierce*' (italics mine), uniting those opposing faculties which in time are fused in Lucy's consciousness. And of course the death of Miss Marchmont's lover in the snow prefigures Monsieur Paul's drowning at sea.

With Miss Marchmont as her paragon, Lucy progresses towards becoming what we call today an 'integrated personality.' Through most of her narrative she makes us aware not only of divisiveness in her own soul, but of the shallowness, defectiveness, or limited spiritual endowments of most of those she meets. Mme Beck, 'wise, firm, faithless; secret, crafty, passionless', represents the *raison* of the French genius, as Monsieur Paul represents its *sensibilité*, and this Lowlands Marquise de Merteuil, gliding through dark rooms with her lantern, rifling drawers furtively in the night, scheming behind her cold, calm visage, is surely as vivid an image as literature offers us of the intellect divorced from passion, unthawed by sentiment, unrefined by sensibility and narrowed by its self-centredness.

Ginevra Fanshawe and Paulina de Bassompierre, the two rivals for the affections of Dr John (once Lucy realizes that she herself is 'out of the running') are judged mainly in terms of the aesthetic virtues, and here it is clear that the Golden Apple is awarded to Polly. Of Miss Fanshawe, Lucy observes early in the novel: 'many a time since have I noticed in persons of . . . light, careless temperament and fair, fragile style of beauty, an entire incapacity to endure. They seem to sour in adversity, like small beer in thunder.' Miss Fanshawe's beauty, Lucy would have us know, is insubstantial—without intellectual or spiritual dimension. She is depicted as a creature dominated by emotion and appetite. As for Polly, Lucy observes: 'The fineness of her beauty, the soft courtesy of her manner, her immature but real and inbred tact,' and notes that 'in letters, in arts, in actual life . . . it soon appeared that she had both read and reflected'. Polly, in other words, possesses mind, manners, morals, *and* personal appearance (to re-apply Monsieur Paul's categories). While Ginevra 'perhaps boasted the advantage in material charms,' Polly 'shone pre-eminent for attractions more subtle and spiritual'.

Much this same psychological contrast—between the material and the spiritual, between outward elegance and inward moral beauty—is made by Lucy in assessing the virtues of the two men in her life—Dr John Bretton, with whom she is briefly infatuated, and Monsieur Paul Emanuel, with whom she falls in love. Lucy's giving up a love 'born of beauty' as represented by Dr John, for another love 'consolidated by affection's pure and durable alloy . . . and finally wrought up, by his own process to his own unflawed completeness' signalizes of course her growing preference for the attributes of nature over those of art. At the same time her 'romantic' love Dr John proves to be limited in his emotional and spiritual range, while her 'real' love Monsieur Paul turns out to have a fuller and more capacious soul. At one point, Lucy, noticing Dr John's indifference to the performance of Vashti that has moved her so deeply, concludes: 'His natural attitude was not the meditative, nor his natural mood the sentimental; *impressionable* he was as dimpling water, but, almost as water, *unimpressible*.' (Italics in original) Dr John's blandness and superficiality prepare her to appreciate Monsieur Paul's intensity and depth. She finds that Monsieur Paul, unlike Dr John, has sympathetic imagination. He had the power to gaze 'deep through the pupil and the iris into the brain . . .'; at other times, when he was conscious of giving pain, 'words can hardly do justice to his tenderness and helpfulness. His own eyes would moisten when tears of shame and effort clouded mine . . . ' Lucy's feelings for Monsieur Paul move from fear, to awed respect, to admiration, to love as she discovers the profundity of his mind and sensibility. At the outset she thinks of him as an irascible, intellectual bully, morally corrupt like his cousin Mme Beck, and a casuist in religion, like the Jesuit Père Silas. But as her coldness towards him diminishes, she discovers his wholeness and integrity of character. By contrast with the other professors she meets, who represent the negative virtues of freedom and independence, 'emancipated free-thinkers, infidels, atheists, and many of them men whose lives would not bear scrutiny,' Lucy recognizes in Monsieur Paul a truly emancipated spirit, one with 'vivid passions, keen feelings . . . pure honour and . . . artless piety . . .'

Through the awakening and invigorating influence of Monsieur Paul, Lucy herself achieves the harmony of soul she admires in him. Earlier in the novel she is obviously in conflict with herself. She is attracted to Dr John aesthetically, but finds herself incompatible with him spiritually. She admires Mme Beck's intellect and efficiency, while finding her repulsive morally. She holds debates with herself wherein her reason argues against her emotions, while at other times her fancy betrays her into delusions which her good sense later corrects. This division in Lucy's soul reflects itself also in the various aspects in which she appears to other people: 'learned and blue' to Mme Beck; 'caustic, ironic and cynical' to Ginevra Fanshawe; 'the pink and pattern of governess correctness' to Mr Home, Polly's father; but to Monsieur Paul 'a fiery and rash nature adventurous, indocile and audacious'. This nature is, of course, subdued and controlled by the Professor. By her last meeting and parting with Monsieur Paul, Lucy indicates through her complete assent to him how her inner nature has arrived at a state of peace with itself: 'Once—unknown and unloved, I held him harsh and strange; the low stature, the wiry make, the angles, the darkness, the manner displeased me. Now, penetrated with his influence, and living by his affection, having his worth by intellect, and his goodness by heart, I preferred him above all humanity.' Here Monsieur Paul's 'mind, morals, manners, personal appearance' are spiritualized.

This vivid psychology, making us continuously aware of a mind reacting to the outside world, has a purpose beyond setting a group of characters before our eyes. Through her most complex heroine, Charlotte Brontë obviously means to depict something of the creative act itself. . . .

One of the most vividly realized of the earlier episodes of *Villette* is that nightmarish sequence ('The Long Vacation'; 'Auld Lang Syne') where Lucy, left alone at the Pension during the Long Vacation, wanders, delirious from fever, through the streets of the city, unburdens herself by confession to the first priest she meets, Père Silas, faints, wakes up to find herself in what looks like the Bretton household where she had spent her happier girlhood. Gradually she recognizes that she has not been transported on a magic carpet to England, but that the Brettons have transported themselves bodily to Labassecour. So, fancy, that 'mode of memory emancipated from the order of time and space', as Coleridge puts it, coalesces with concrete association—and this incident may be taken as emblematic of what happens in the course of the novel to Lucy's imagination. The nocturnal part of her mind conjures up ghosts of nuns in the *berceau*. It wanders opium-dazed through the midnight *fête* of the Haute-Ville, where all those who have played their parts in her life are illuminated in a phantasmagoria of flambeaux, lamps, and torches. But this is the state of mind that Coleridge termed 'delirium,' where fancy runs riot and beyond the control of reason. It is in the natural light of day, when reason gains control, that Lucy learns the truth about Monsieur Paul, and discovers her profound love for him.

The very love of Lucy Snowe and Paul Emanuel seems itself to represent the great syncretical act of the fully operating Creative Imagination: the cold North (note Lucy's last name) thawed by Iberian warmth (Monsieur Paul comes from Spain); English stolidity fused with continental temperament; independent Protestantism united to authoritarian Catholicism; beauty found in ugliness; fear and revulsion growing into love. . . .

With the nun, as with other characters in *Villette*, Charlotte Brontë distorted outmoded literary conventions in a pointedly perverse way. Making the source of the ghost stem from the comic side of the novel —in a prank played by Ginevra's foppish lover de Hamal—is surely the author's way of mocking the tradition that once had teased her own fevered fancy. This, her last word on the Gothic novel, is a laugh at it—and a laugh that liberates. Lucy Snowe, destroying the empty vestments of the nun, is the heroine of the 'new' realistic novel sloughing off the trappings of the shadowy heroine of the 'old' romantic novel. As Lucy Snowe clears her mind of the phantoms from the past that have haunted it, so Charlotte Brontë exorcises the Gothic novel that once fired her imagination, even as Miss Austen had exorcized it earlier in the century.

It is when Lucy returns from the midnight *fête*—the supreme symbolic scene of the novel—to her room in the Pension, Mme Beck's drug having run its course, that she discovers the 'identity' of the nun. While wandering through the masquerade in the Park, where 'so strange a feeling of revelry and mystery began to spread abroad', Lucy for a time expects, and leads the reader to expect, that she will find the nun among these nocturnal figures. But the fancy does not cheat so well, and Lucy abruptly calls us back to ourselves with: 'All falsities—all figments! We will not deal in this gear. Let us be honest, and cut . . . from the homely web of truth.' The supposed nun turns out to be a 'buxom and blooming . . . bourgeois belle'. 'The whole conjuration, the secret junta' are her old acquaintances disporting themselves in bourgeois fashion at a bourgeois carnival. Thus Lucy gradually penetrates this 'woody and turfy theatre', this 'strangest architectural wealth—of altar and temple, of pyramid, obelisk and sphinx', with which Villette is decked out on this carnival night, and recognizes it as false enchantment, as mere overlay of 'timber, paint and pasteboard'. Now comes the cold light of dawn that brings her rendezvous and parting with Monsieur Paul Emanuel.

So once and for all time Lucy Snowe has rid herself of the illusions of fable and theatre, and the romantic imagination reconciles itself to real life. No 'and they lived happily ever after' here. Separation and

sorrow must be endured and lived with in this life. No sudden rise to
social position and the manor house that goes with it—but a decent
competency as mistress of an *externat de demoiselles*. The past returns
to us not as apparition, not in reincarnation, but as memory. And
Life does not punish its villains, either, in the way of the fables and
the romances: 'Madame Beck prospered all the days of her life; so
did Père Silas; Madame Walravens fulfilled her ninetieth year before
she died. Farewell.' Bitterness and irrational passion give way to understanding and acceptance of things as they are.

From '*Villette* and the Life of the Mind,' in *P.M.L.A.,* vol.
LXXV, No. 4, 1960, pp. 410–19.

Critics on Emily Brontë

SYDNEY DOBELL, LADY EASTLAKE, G. H. LEWES

The Early Reviews

The *Poems*

Poems, By C., E. and A. Bell

The second book on our list furnishes another example of a family in whom appears to run the instinct of song. It is shared, however, by the three brothers—as we suppose them to be—in very unequal proportions; requiring, in the case of Acton Bell, the indulgences of affection . . . to make it music,—and rising, in that of Ellis, into an inspiration, which may yet find an audience in the outer world. A fine quaint spirit has the latter, which may have things to speak that men will be glad to hear,—and an evident power of wing that may reach heights not here attempted.

Sydney Dobell, Athenaeum, No. 975, July 4, 1846, pp. 682

Wuthering Heights

. . . At all events there can be no interest attached to the writer of *Wuthering Heights*—a novel succeeding *Jane Eyre*, and purporting to be written by Ellis Bell—unless it were for the sake of more individual reprobation. For though there is a decided family likeness between the two, yet the aspect of the Jane and Rochester animals in their native state, as Catherine and Heathfield, is too odiously and abominably pagan to be palatable even to the most vitated class of English readers. With all the unscrupulousness of the French school of novels it combines that repulsive vulgarity in the choice of its vice which supplies its own antidote. . . .

E. Rigby (Lady Eastlake), *Quarterly Review*, vol. LXXXIV, 1848, p. 175.

. . . Although there is a want of air and light in the picture we cannot deny its truth; sombre, rude, brutal, yet true. The fierce ungoverned instincts of powerful organizations, bred up amidst violence, revolt, and moral apathy, are here seen in operation; such brutes we should all be, or the most of us, were our lives as insubordinate to law; were our affections and sympathies as little cultivated, our imaginations as undirected. And herein lies the moral of the book, though most people will fail to draw the moral from very irritation at it. . . .

The power [of 'vigorous delineation'], indeed, is wonderful. Heathcliff, devil though he be, is drawn with a sort of dusky splendour which fascinates, and we feel the truth of his burning and impassioned love for Catherine, and of her inextinguishable love for him. It was a happy thought to make her love the kind, weak, elegant Edgar, and yet without lessening her passion for Heathcliff. Edgar appeals to her love of refinement, and goodness, and culture: Heathcliff clutches her soul in his passionate embrace. Edgar is the husband she has chosen, the man who alone is fit to call her wife; but although she is ashamed of her early playmate, she loves him with a passionate abandonment which sets culture, education, the world at defiance. It is in the treatment of this subject that Ellis Bell shows real mastery, and it shows more genius, in the highest sense of the word, than you will find in a thousand novels. . . .

G. H. Lewes, The Leader, December 28, 1850, p. 953.

CHARLOTTE BRONTË

Wuthering Heights

I have just read over *Wuthering Heights,* and, for the first time, have obtained a clear glimpse of what are termed (and, perhaps, really are) its faults; have gained a definite notion of how it appears to other people—to strangers who knew nothing of the author; who are unacquainted with the locality where the scenes of the story are laid; to whom the inhabitants, the customs, the natural characteristics of the outlying hills and hamlets in the West Riding of Yorkshire are things alien and unfamiliar.

To all such, *Wuthering Heights* must appear a rude and strange production. The wild moors of the north of England can for them have no interest; the language, the manners, the very dwellings and household customs of the scattered inhabitants of those districts, must be to such readers in a great measure unintelligible, and—where intelligible—repulsive. Men and women who, perhaps naturally very calm, and with feelings moderate in degree. and little marked in kind, have been trained from their cradle to observe the utmost evenness of manner and guardedness of language, will hardly know what to make of the rough, strong utterance, the harshly manifested passions, the unbridled aversions, and headlong partialities of unlettered moorland hinds and rugged moorland squires, who have grown up untaught and unchecked, except by mentors as harsh as themselves. . . .

With regard to the rusticity of *Wuthering Heights,* I admit the charge, for I feel the quality. It is rustic all through. It is moorish, and wild, and knotty as a root of heath. Nor was it natural that it should be otherwise; the author being herself a native and nursling of the moors. Doubtless, had her lot been cast in a town, her writings, if she had written at all, would have possessed another character. Even had chance or taste led her to choose a similar subject, she would have treated it otherwise. Had Ellis Bell been a lady or a gentleman accustomed to what is called 'the world,' her view of a remote and unreclaimed region, as well as of the dwellers therein, would have differed greatly from that actually taken by the home-bred country girl. Doubtless it would have been wider—more comprehensive: whether it would have been more original or more truthful is not so certain. As far as the scenery and locality are concerned, it could scarcely have been so sympathetic: Ellis Bell did not describe as one whose eyes and taste alone found pleasure in the prospect; her native hills were far more to her than a spectacle; they were what she lived in, and by, as much as the wild birds, their tenants, or as the heather, their produce. Her descriptions, then, of natural scenery, are what they should be, and all they should be.

Where delineation of human character is concerned, the case is different. I am bound to avow that she had scarcely more practical knowledge of the peasantry amongst whom she lived than a nun has of the country people who sometimes pass her convent gates. My sister's disposition was not naturally gregarious; circumstances favoured and fostered her tendency to seclusion; except to go to church or take a walk on the hills, she rarely crossed the threshold of home. Though her feeling for the people round was benevolent, intercourse with them she never sought; nor, with very few exceptions, ever experienced. And yet she knew them: knew their ways, their language, their family histories; she could hear of them with interest, and talk of them with detail, minute, graphic, and accurate; but *with* them, she rarely exchanged a word. Hence it ensued that what her mind had gathered of the real concerning them was too exclusively confined to those tragic and terrible traits of which, in listening to the secret annals of every rude vicinage, the memory is sometimes compelled to receive the impress. Her imagination, which was a spirit more sombre than sunny, more powerful than sportive, found in such traits material whence it wrought creations like Heathcliff, like Earnshaw, like Catherine. Having formed these beings she did not know what she had done. If the auditor of her work, when read in manuscript, shuddered under the grinding influence of natures so relentless and implacable, of spirits so lost and fallen; if it was complained that the mere hearing of certain vivid and fearful scenes banished sleep by night, and disturbed mental peace by day, Ellis Bell would wonder what was meant, and suspect the complainant of affectation. Had she but lived, her mind would of itself have grown like a strong tree, loftier, straighter, wider-spreading, and its matured fruits would have attained a mellower ripeness and sunnier bloom; but on that mind time and experience alone could work: to the influence of other intellects, it was not amenable.

Having avowed that over much of *Wuthering Heights* there broods 'a horror of great darkness'; that, in its storm-heated and electrical atmosphere, we seem at times to breathe lightning, let me point to those spots where clouded daylight and the eclipsed sun still attest their existence. For a specimen of true benevolence and homely fidelity, look at the character of Nelly Dean; for an example of constancy and tenderness, remark that of Edgar Linton. (Some people will think these qualities do not shine so well incarnate in a man as they would do in a woman, but Ellis Bell could never be brought to comprehend this notion: nothing moved her more than any insinuation that the faithfulness and clemency, the long-suffering and loving-kindness which are esteemed virtues in the daughters of Eve, become foibles in the sons of Adam. She held that mercy and forgiveness are the divinest attributes of the Great Being who made both man and woman, and that what clothes the Godhead in glory, can disgrace no form of feeble humanity.) There is a dry, saturnine humour in the delineation of old Joseph, and some glimpses of grace and gaiety animate the younger Catherine. Nor is even the first heroine of the name destitute of a certain strange beauty in her fierceness, or of honesty in the midst of perverted passion and passionate perversity.

Heathcliff, indeed, stands unredeemed; never once swerving in his arrow-straight course to perdition, from the time when 'the little black-haired swarthy thing, as dark as if it came from the Devil', was first unrolled out of the bundle and set on its feet in the farmhouse kitchen, to the hour when Nelly Dean found the grim, stalwart corpse laid on its back in the panel-enclosed bed, with wide-gazing eyes that seemed 'to sneer at her attempt to close them, and parted lips and sharp white teeth that sneered too.'

Heathcliff betrays one solitary human feeling, and that is *not* his love for Catherine; which is a sentiment fierce and inhuman; a passion such as might boil and glow in the bad essence of some evil genius; a fire that might form the tormented centre—the ever-suffering soul of a magnate of the infernal world: and by its quenchless and ceaseless ravage effect the execution of the decree which dooms him to carry Hell with him wherever he wanders. No; the single link that connects Heathcliff with humanity is his rudely confessed regard for Hareton Earnshaw—the young man whom he has ruined; and then his half-implied esteem for Nelly Dean. These solitary traits omitted, we should say he was child neither of Lascar nor gipsy, but a man's shape animated by demon life—a Ghoul—an Afreet.

Whether it is right or advisable to create beings like Heathcliff, I do not know: I scarcely think it is. But this I know: the writer who possesses the creative gift owns something of which he is not always master—something that, at times, strangely wills and works for itself. . . .

Wuthering Heights was hewn in a wild workshop, with simple tools, out of homely materials. The statuary found a granite block on a solitary moor; gazing thereon, he saw how from the crag might be elicited a head, savage, swart, sinister; a form moulded with at least one element of grandeur—power. He wrought with a rude chisel, and from no model but the vision of his meditations. With time and labour, the crag took human shape; and there it stands colossal, dark, and frowning, half-statue, half rock: in the former sense, terrible and goblin-like; in the latter, almost beautiful, for its colouring is of mellow grey, and moorland moss clothes it; and heath, with its blooming bells and balmy fragrance, grows faithfully close to the giant's foot.

The Editor's Preface to the second edition of *Wuthering Heights*,
Smith Elder, London, 1850.

VIRGINIA WOOLF

Wuthering Heights

. . . The meaning of a book, which lies so often apart from what happens and what is said and consists rather in some connection which things in themselves different have had for the writer, is necessarily hard to grasp. Especially this is so when, like the Brontës, the writer is poetic, and his meaning inseparable from his language, and itself rather a mood than a particular observation. *Wuthering Heights* is a more difficult book to understand than *Jane Eyre*, because Emily was a greater poet than Charlotte. When Charlotte wrote she said with eloquence and splendour and passion 'I love', 'I hate', 'I suffer'.

Her experience, though more intense, is on a level with our own. But there is no 'I' in *Wuthering Heights*. There are no governesses. There are no employers. There is love, but it is not the love of men and women. Emily was inspired by some more general conception. The impulse which urged her to create was not her own suffering or her own injuries. She looked out upon a world cleft into gigantic disorder and felt within her the power to unite it in a book. That gigantic ambition is to be felt throughout the novel—a struggle, half thwarted but of superb conviction, to say something through the mouths of her characters which is not merely 'I love' or 'I hate', but 'we, the whole human race' and 'you, the eternal powers...' the sentence remains unfinished. It is not strange that it should be so; rather it is astonishing that she can make us feel what she had it in her to say at all. It surges up in the half-articulate words of Catherine Earnshaw, 'If all else perished and *he* remained, I should still continue to be; and if all else remained and he were annihilated, the universe would turn to a mighty stranger; I should not seem part of it'. It breaks out again in the presence of the dead. 'I see a repose that neither earth nor hell can break, and I feel an assurance of the endless and shadowless hereafter—the eternity they have entered—where life is boundless in its duration, and love in its sympathy and joy in its fullness.' It is this suggestion of power underlying the apparitions of human nature and lifting them up into the presence of greatness that gives the book its huge stature among other novels....

It is as if she could tear up all that we know human beings by, and fill these unrecognizable transparences with such a gust of life that they transcend reality. Hers, then, is the rarest of all powers. She could free life from its dependence on facts; with a few touches indicate the spirit of a face so that it needs no body; by speaking of the moor make the wind blow and the thunder roar.

From '*Jane Eyre* and *Wuthering Heights*', in *The Common Reader*, Hogarth Press, London, 1925; 2nd ed. 1929, pp. 196–204. The essay was written in 1916.

C. P. SANGER

The Structure of *Wuthering Heights*

How is a long story like this to be told? How is the reader's interest to be excited? How is the tale to be kept together? How are we to be made to feel the lapse of time without being pestered by dates?

How far did the authoress accurately visualize the ages of the characters in the different incidents, the topography, and so on? And how
did Heathcliff succeed in getting the property? These are the questions I attempt to answer.

The most obvious thing about the structure of the story which
deals with three generations is the symmetry of the pedigree. Mr and
Mrs Earnshaw at Wuthering Heights and Mr and Mrs Linton at
Thrushcross Grange each have one son and one daughter. Mr
Linton's son marries Mr Earnshaw's daughter, and their only child
Catherine marries successively her two cousins—Mr Linton's grandson
and Mr Earnshaw's grandson. See the following pedigree:—

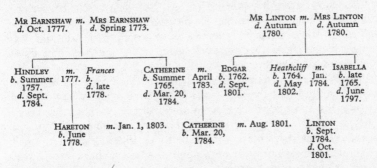

MR EARNSHAW *m.* MRS EARNSHAW   MR LINTON *m.* MRS LINTON
d. Oct. 1777. | *d.* Spring 1773.   *d.* Autumn | *d.* Autumn
                                          1780.   1780.

HINDLEY   *m.* *Frances*   CATHERINE   *m.*   EDGAR   *Heathcliff* *m.* ISABELLA
b. Summer 1777. *b.*   *b.* Summer April *b.* 1762. *b.* 1764. Jan. *b.* late
1757.   *d.* late   1765.   1783. *d.* Sept.   *d.* May   1784. 1765.
d. Sept.   1778.   *d.* Mar. 20,   1801.   1802.   *d.* June
1784.   1784.   1797.

HARETON   *m.* Jan. 1, 1803.   CATHERINE   *m.* Aug. 1801.   LINTON
b. June   *b.* Mar. 20,   *b.* Sept.
1778.   1784.   1784.
                                                              d. Oct.
                                                              1801.

In actual life I have never come across a pedigree of such absolute
symmetry. I shall have to refer to this pedigree again later. It is a
remarkable piece of symmetry in a tempestuous book.

The method adopted to arouse the reader's interest and to give vividness and reality to the tale is one which has been used with great
success by Joseph Conrad. But it requires great skill.

After Edgar Linton's death, Mr Lockwood, the narrator, takes
Thrushcross Grange for a year. He goes to call on his landlord,
Heathcliff, at Wuthering Heights, and is puzzled to find there a
farouche young woman and an awkward boor. At first he supposes
Catherine to be Heathcliff's wife; when told she is his daughter-in-law,
he then supposes that Hareton is Heathcliff's son, and has again to
be corrected. He, and the reader, are naturally puzzled at this strange
trio. Lockwood calls again, and is forced to spend the night because
of a heavy fall of snow. In his room he finds some books with the
name Catherine Earnshaw and Catherine Linton, and a sort of diary
of Catherine's in a childish hand which gives a vivid picture of the
situation just after her father's death. Mr Lockwood has a nightmare in which Catherine's spirit comes to the window, and he also
witnesses a strange scene of Heathcliff imploring Catherine's spirit.
Our interest cannot fail now to be excited. What is this strange man

and this strange menage? Who was this Catherine who died years before? What were her relations with Heathcliff? Naturally, Lockwood is much intrigued. On his way back next day he catches a chill and becomes ill. To pass the time he asks Ellen Dean, the housekeeper at Thrushcross Grange, what she knows about the family at Wuthering Heights. She, who was the first Hareton's nurse and then the younger Catherine's, tells him the story of the past thirty years in considerable detail. So that during the major part of the book Mr Lockwood is telling us what Ellen Dean told him, but sometimes, also, what Ellen Dean told him that someone else—for instance, Isabella—had told her. Only a small part, perhaps one-tenth of the book, consists of direct narrative by Lockwood from his own knowledge. But such a scheme may be confusing, and it is easy to muddle the time. Did Emily Brontë realize and let us know the dates when each event happened? She did, but not by giving them directly. Look again at the pedigree. The dates there have all been derived from the book, yet only one is directly stated. What first brought me to study the book more closely was when I noticed that the first word in the book was a date—1801. I thought this must have some significance. Similarly, the first word of Chapter XXXII is 1802. Apart from this, only one other date is given directly. In the last sentence of Chapter VII, Ellen Dean says, 'I will be content to pass on to the next summer—the summer of 1778, that is, nearly twenty-three years ago'. This gives no further information, as 1801 is twenty-three years after 1778, but in the first sentence of the next chapter she tells us that Hareton was born in June. This is how I get June 1778 for Hareton's birth in the pedigree. But what about the rest of the dates, not only those in the pedigree but of all the incidents in the story? There are a considerable number (perhaps nearly a hundred) indications of various kinds to help us—intervals of time, ages of characters, the months, the harvest moon, the last grouse, and so forth, and we learn, incidentally, that the younger Catherine's birthday was on March 20th. Sometimes, too, we know the day of the week—thus Ellen Dean will remember something which happened on a Sunday, or on a Christmas Eve. Taking all these indications, it is, I think, possible to ascertain this year, and, in most cases, the month of the year in which every event takes place—also the ages of the various characters, except, naturally, there is a slight doubt as to Heathcliff, because no one knows his exact age when he was found by Mr Earnshaw. But one has to go warily and consider all the indications together, for there is a curious subtlety that sometimes the characters are described as *looking* some ages which are not exact. Thus Lockwood when he first describes them says that Heathcliff was about forty and Catherine did not look seventeen. In fact, Catherine was seventeen and three-quarters and Heathcliff cannot have been more than thirty-eight. It would be too tedious to state the process by which I have discovered each date. But I will give one or two illustrations. We already know that Hareton was born in June 1778; we are told that he was nearly five when Catherine Earnshaw married Edgar Linton, so that the marriage was before June 1783. But Heathcliff returned in September after they had been happily married for six months. Thus the marriage was in April 1783. We are told that the scene that led to Catherine's death was a Sunday in the March after Heathcliff's return, and that her daughter, Catherine, was born about midnight, and the mother died two hours after. Later on we learn that Catherine's birthday was the 20th (and that this was also treated as the day of her mother's death). Hence Catherine died at 2 a.m. on Monday, March 20, 1784.

I will give only one other instance. Lockwood begins his account in 1801; it is snowy weather, which might be in January or February or in November or December. But he returns in 1802 before his year's tenancy is out. Hence the story begins at the end of 1801. A Michaelmas tenancy begins on October 10th—not on September 29th—because when the calendar was reformed eleven days were left out. Therefore, the story begins after October 10, 1801. Now after Lockwood has been ill three weeks Heathcliff sends him some grouse, the last of the season. Since the Game Act, 1831, grouse may not be shot after December 10th, so we may take this as about the date for the last grouse. Thus the story begins about the middle of November, and this fits pretty well with the later indications. That is sufficient to illustrate the process. Sometimes it is only by fitting together several indications, each rather vague, that one can find the month. There is, however, one curious fact. We can ascertain Hindley's age. Now Ellen Dean was of the same age. She was his foster sister, and the doctor also refers to her as being of the same age as Hindley. Yet she makes two mistakes about her own age. Middle-aged people do, of course, make mistakes about their age, and these slips may have been intentional on the part of Emily Brontë, but, if so, it seems to me a little over-subtle.

The topography is equally precise. On going from Thrushcross Grange to the village of Gimmerton a highway branches off to the moor on the left. There is a stone pillar there. Thrushcross Grange lies to the south-west, Gimmerton to the east, and Wuthering Heights to the north. The distance from Thrushcross Grange to Wuthering Heights is four miles, and Penistone Crags lie a mile and a half farther on. It was half an hour from Gimmerton to Thrushcross Grange.

The botany is sure to be correct. Emily Brontë loved the country. I was a little surprised to find an ash tree in bud as early as March 20th, but then I realized that it was not on the moor but in the park at

Thrushcross Grange, which lay low and was no doubt sheltered.

I now come to the final problem. Heathcliff schemed to get all the property of both the Earnshaws and the Lintons. How did he do it? Emily Brontë clearly had a considerable knowledge of the law. . . . [*C. P. Sanger goes on to explain the law of entails and the legal technicalities of the problem. He shows how, by the time of his death, Heathcliff is the mortgagee in possession of Wuthering Heights and also, though wrongfully, in possession of Thrushcross Grange. On his death Catherine inherits Thrushcross Grange and Hareton gets Wuthering Heights.*]

There is, so far as I know, no other novel in the world which it is possible to subject to an analysis of the kind I have tried to make. This in itself makes the book very unusual. Did the authoress carry all the dates in her head, or did she work with a calendar? Was March 20, 1784, for example, on a Monday? According to my calculations it was not, it was a Saturday, but I should like to have this confirmed by some competent chronologist; for if I am right, it shows that Emily Brontë did not use a calendar, and that nothing will be gained by finding out, for instance, the date of Easter in 1803.

However dull and technical the above details may be, they do, I believe, throw a light on the character of Emily Brontë and her book. German romances can hardly have been the source of her knowledge of English law. A great critic has spoken of the passionate chastity of the book; but the extreme care in realizing the ages of the characters at the time of each incident which is described seems to me a more unusual characteristic of a novel. It demonstrates the vividness of the author's imagination.

From *The Structure of 'Wuthering Heights'*, Hogarth Essays, No. 19, Hogarth Press, London, 1921, pp. 8–14, 19–20. University Microfilms, Inc., Anne Arbor and London.

[This classic essay by C. P. Sanger, a Chancery barrister of Lincoln's Inn, was published under the initials C. P. S. In an appendix to the essay the author gives a detailed chronology of the events in the novel.]

IRENE COOPER-WILLIS

The Style of *Wuthering Heights*

. . . Now take the indoors scene and notice how the paint, so to speak, is put on there. [See Chapter I. Please find and read the whole passage]

One step brought us into the family sitting-room, without any
introductory lobby or passage. . . .
In an arch under the dresser, reposed a huge, liver-coloured bitch
pointer, surrounded by a swarm of squealing puppies; and other
dogs haunted other recesses.

Observe the straightness of the direction of the first sentence—'One
step brought us into the family sitting-room'—it marches exactly with
the action it describes. Again, see how verbs of movement are used
about things which in themselves are motionless, and how, by a
change of mood of the verb, from active to passive, variety of movement and also spatial dimension are suggested. 'The kitchen is *forced
to retreat*'—'one or two heavy black ones [chairs] *lurking* in the
shade'—'ranks of immense pewter dishes . . . *towering*'. The roof is
given personality; its anatomy is spoken of. Another substantial effect
is produced upon the reader by direct emphasis upon Lockwood's
visual and audible impressions, 'a chatter of tongues'; 'a clatter of
culinary utensils'; 'light and heat from ranks of immense pewter
dishes'. All this is astonishingly dramatic, yet it does not affect us
astonishingly, until we come to examine the structure; in reading it in
the ordinary way, we feel merely that we are in close contact with
the scene. The technique is as effective as the craft of the stage-
furniture maker, who has to cut all decorative detail much more deeply
than it would be cut for everyday use, in order that it may be seen
at a distance from the front of the stage—where it merely looks like
ordinary furniture.

Equally effective is the way in which, in the scene of the distur-
bance when Lockwood is set upon by the dogs and has to be rescued
by the cook, we are made to realize his discomfort and gradual
return to composure. . . .

In those [introductory] chapters, Lockwood, the diarist, is facing
the immediate present, is *barging* into it, to use a vulgar expression,
but one which happens to fit the way he behaves on his visits to the
farm. He cannot see ahead; there is no time dimension to reckon with
in describing his experience; all that he is concerned to convey to
the reader is what is taking place where, at the moment, he is. But in
the main part of the book, the present is *behind* Lockwood; he is looking the other way, under Mrs Dean's guidance, across and through a
long period of years. It is not enough that he should see past scenes
vividly; his attention must also be guided to crucial, determining
events. The seizure of these, the emphasis placed on their relationship
to each other, and on the links between them, is the equivalent, in a
survey of the past, of that accent upon movement which, in the
description of a scene, is essential to make it vivid. Crucial events, in

short, may be regarded as the hinges of action in a story, and cogency and stress upon these are the incisive tools with which a writer must work, if the story is to be dramatically told. . . .

From *The Authorship of 'Wuthering Heights'*, Hogarth Press, London, 1936, pp. 22–5, 43.

DEREK TRAVERSI

Emily Brontë's Romanticism

. . . The romantic melodramas with which Emily Brontë was certainly familiar owed their success precisely to effects created by ambiguity and mistiness, lack of precision and vague suggestiveness. The power to rouse in the reader emotions of fear or horror was, in work of this kind, directly proportionate to the lack of definition which the authors were careful to impart to their descriptions. Romantic emotion of this type is always felt rather than seen, is always rather a possible happening than a present and tangible reality. In *Wuthering Heights*, on the contrary, the exact opposite occurs. Although the events described may strike us on occasions as incredible, they are related almost invariably with an unmistakable and vivid clarity. The qualities by which the book is differentiated from the commonplaces of romantic sensibility are nowhere more apparent than in the opening description of Heathcliff's house and its surroundings. Wuthering Heights is described, as Mr Lockwood sees it, in a series of vivid and exact touches. The exposition, careful, orderly, and even slightly pedantic, as befits the speaker, rises almost imperceptibly to the deeply poetic reference to 'the range of gaunt thorns all stretching their limbs one way, as if craving alms of the sun', so that this evocation does not strike the reader as in any way unjustified or merely a poetic intrusion. Above all, the temptation to exploit the poetic note thus introduced, and so to diminish its effectiveness, is firmly resisted and the description of the interior of the house which follows, as precise in detail as it is appreciative in tone and careful to stress the normality of the setting ('The apartment and furniture would have been nothing extraordinary as belonging to a homely northern farmer'), reveals a type of writing diametrically opposed to the romantic sensationalism which the authoress might so easily have derived from her natural models. The same firm grasp of the concrete detail is apparent a few pages further on even in Mr Lockwood's account of his highly theatrical dream, where if anywhere we might have expected the strained

romantic note to impose a suitable lack of precision, but where in fact
the illusion of reality is conveyed with an immediate sense of physical
pain that borders on the intolerable: 'Terror made me cruel; and,
finding it useless to attempt shaking the creature off, *I pulled its wrist
on to the broken pane, and rubbed it to and fro* till the blood ran
and soaked the bedclothes'. In such a passage the peculiar intensity
of Emily Brontë's romanticism—if we may use the word for lack of a
better—even though working on conventional material achieves its
effect through a remarkable and characteristic concreteness. It was the
capacity to effect an intimate fusion between the thing seen or the felt
sensation, and its imaginative interpretation, to unite the immediate
and concrete with the intensity of feeling proper to poetry that
enabled her to raise a melodramatic theme to the level of a profoundly
personal creation. . . .

From 'Wuthering Heights After a Hundred Years', The Dublin
Review, vol. 222, No. 445, 1949, pp. 154–68.

MARK SCHORER

The Metaphors in *Wuthering Heights*

. . . *Wuthering Heights*, as I understand it, means to be a work of
edification: Emily Brontë begins by wishing to instruct her narrator,
the dandy, Lockwood, in the nature of a grand passion; she ends by
instructing herself in the vanity of human wishes. She means to dramatize with something like approval—the phrase that follows is from
Middlemarch—'the sense of a stupendous self and an insignificant
world'. What her metaphors signify is the impermanence of self and
the permanence of something larger.

To exalt the power of human feeling, Emily Brontë roots her
analogies in the fierce life of animals and in the relentless life of the
elements—fire, wind, water. 'Wuthering', we are told, is 'a significant
provincial adjective, descriptive of the atmospheric tumult to which
its station is exposed in stormy weather', and, immediately after, that
'one may guess the power of the north wind blowing over the edge,
by the excessive slant of a few stunted firs at the end of the house;
and by a range of gaunt thorns all stretching their limbs one way, as
if craving alms of the sun'. The application of this landscape to the
characters is made explicit in the second half of the novel, when
Heathcliff says, 'Now, my bonny lad, you are *mine*! And we'll see
if one tree won't grow as crooked as another, with the same wind to

twist it!' This analogy provides at least half of the metaphorical base of the novel.

Human conditions are like the activities of the landscape, where rains *flood,* blasts *wail,* and the snow and wind *whirl wildly* and *blow* out lights. A serving woman *heaves* 'like a sea after a high wind'; a preacher '*poured* forth his zeal in a *shower*'; Mrs Dean *rushes* to welcome Lockwood, 'exclaiming *tumultuously*'; spirits are 'at high-water mark'; Linton's soul is as different from Heathcliff's 'as a moon-beam from lightning, or frost from fire'; abuse is *lavished* in a *torrent,* or *pours forth* in a *deluge;* illnesses are '*weathered* . . . through'; 'sensa-tions' are felt in a *gush;* 'your veins are *full* of *ice water;* but mine are *boiling*'; hair *flies,* bodies *toss* or *tremble* like reeds, tears *stream* or *rain down* among ashes; discord and distress arise in a *tumult;* Catherine Linton 'was *struck* during a *tempest* of passion with a kind of fit' and '*flew off* in the *height* of it'.

Faces, too, are like landscapes: 'a *cloud* of meditation' hangs over Nelly Dean's *ruddy* countenance'; Catherine had 'a suddenly *clouded* brow; her humour was a mere *vane* for constantly varying caprices'; 'the surface of' the boy Heathcliff's 'face and hands was dismally *beclouded*' with dirt; later, his face '*brightened* for a moment; then it was *overcast* afresh'. 'His forehead . . . *shaded* over with a heavy *cloud';* and 'the *clouded* windows of hell', his eyes, '*flashed*'. Hareton, likewise, grows 'black as a *thundercloud*'; or *darkens* with a frown. The older Catherine experienced whole '*seasons* of gloom', and the younger Catherine's 'heart was *clouded* . . . in double *darkness*'. Her 'face was just like the *landscape—shadows* and *sunshine* flitting over it in rapid succession; but the *shadows* rested longer, and the *sun-shine* was more transient'. Sometimes 'her eyes are *radiant* with *cloudless* pleasure', and at the end, Hareton shakes off 'the *clouds* of ignorance and degradation', and his '*brightening* mind *brightened* his features'.

Quite as important as the imagery of wind and cloud and water is the imagery of fire. In every interior, the fire on the hearth is the centre of pictorial interest, and the characters sit '*burning* their eyes out before the fire'. Eyes *burn* with anguish but do not *melt;* they always *flash* and *sparkle.* Fury *kindles,* temper *kindles,* a '*spark* of spirit' *kindles.* Catherine has a *fiery* disposition, but so do objects and states: words *brand,* shame is *burning,* merriment *expires* quickly, fevers *consume* life; hot coffee and basins *smoke,* they do not steam; and Isabella shrieks 'as if witches were running *red-hot* needles into her'. Sometimes fire is identified with other elements, as when a servant urges '*flakes* of *flame* up the chimney', or when Isabella com-plains that the fire causes the wound on her neck, first stopped by the icy cold, to stream and smart.

Metaphors of earth—earth takes more solid and durable forms than the other elements—are interestingly few. Twice Heathcliff is likened to 'an arid wilderness of *furze* and *whinstone*'; there is a reference to his '*flinty* gratification'; and once he speaks scornfully of 'the *soil* of' Linton's 'shallow cares'. Earth and vegetation sometimes result in a happy juxtaposition of the vast or the violent and the little or the homely, as when Heathcliff says of Linton that 'He might as well plant *an oak in a flower-pot*', or when he threatens to 'crush his ribs in like *a rotten hazelnut*', which is like his saying that Catherine's passion could be as readily encompassed by Linton as '*the sea* could be . . . contained in that *horse-trough*'.

Most of the animals are wild. Hareton's 'whiskers encroached *bearishly* over his cheeks', and Heathcliff denies the paternity of 'that bear'. Hareton had been 'cast out like an unfledged *dunnock*', and Heathcliff is a 'fierce, pitiless, *wolfish* man'. He is also 'a *bird* of bad omen' and 'an evil *beast*' prowling between a 'stray *sheep*' 'and the fold, waiting his time to spring and destroy'. He has a '*ferocious* gaze' and a '*savage* utterance'; he *growls* and *howls* 'like a beast', and is many times named 'a brute', 'a beast', 'a brute beast'. He struggles like a *bear*, he has *sharp cannibal teeth* which *gleam* 'through the dark', and '*basilisk* eyes . . . *quenched* by sleeplessness'. He *gnashes* his teeth and *foams* like a *mad dog*. He is 'like a *bull*' to Linton's '*lamb*', and only at the very end, the exhausted end, 'he breathed as fast as a *cat*'.

For the domestic and the gentler animals are generally used for purposes of harsh satire or vilification. Edgar, 'the soft thing', 'possessed the power to depart, as much as a *cat* possesses the power to leave a *mouse* half killed, or a *bird* half eaten'. He is 'not a *lamb*' but 'a sucking *leveret*', and his sister is a 'pitiful, slavish, mean-minded *brach*', she is among those *worms*, who, 'the more they writhe, the more' Heathcliff yearns 'to crush out their entrails'. Hindley dies in a stupor, 'snorting like a *horse*'; 'flaying and scalping' would not have roused him, and when the doctor arrives, 'the *beast* has changed to *carrion*'. Hareton is 'an infernal *calf*', and young Linton is a '*puling chicken*' and a '*whelp*'. Like a dying dog, he 'slowly *trailed* himself off, and lay down', or, like a cold one, he '*shrank* closer to the fire'. He 'had *shrunk* into a corner of the settle, as quiet as a *mouse*'; he is called 'a little perishing *monkey*'; and he 'achieved his exist exactly as a *spaniel* might'. He is also 'an abject *reptile*' and 'a *cockatrice*'. Hareton, who is capable on occasion of gathering '*venom* with reflection', is once called a '*magpie*', and once said to be 'obstinate as a *mule*'—one of the few kindly animal references in the novel. To be sure, Isabella describes herself as though she were a deer: 'I *bounded, leaped* and *flew* down the steep road, then . . . *shot* direct across the moor, *rolling* over banks, and *wading* through marshes'. And Catherine, on the whole, is not abused. She is a 'cunning little *fox*' and she runs 'like a *mouse*', but chiefly she is 'soft and mild as a *dove*'.

Emily Brontë's metaphors colour all her diction. As her epithets are charged with passion—'jealous guardianship', 'vexatious phlegm', 'importunate branch'—so her verbs are verbs of violent movement and conflict, both contributing to a rhetorical texture where everything is at a pitch from which it can only subside. The verbs *demand* exhaustion, just as the metaphors *demand* rest. And there is an antithetical chorus in this rhetoric, a contrapuntal warning, which, usually but not only in the voice of Nelly Dean, says, 'Hush! Hush!' all through the novel, at the beginning of paragraph after paragraph. At the end, everything *is* hushed. And the moths *fluttering* over Heathcliff's grave and 'the soft wind *breathing* through the grass' that grows on it have at last more power than he, for all his passion. These soft and fragile things paradoxically endure.

The passions of animals, if we may speak of them as passions, have meaning in that they are presumably necessary to survival; Heathcliff's passion destroys others, himself, and at last, itself. The tumult of the elements alternates with periods of peace, and the seasons are not only autumn and winter. The *fact* of alternation enables nature to endure. The singleness of Heathcliff's tempestuous and wintry emotional life dooms it. Thus there is a curious and ironic contrast between the condition and the destiny of Heathcliff, and the full facts of those areas of metaphor. When, at the end of the novel, Nelly remarks that 'the same moon shone through the window; and the same autumn landscape lay outside' as eighteen years before, she is speaking with metaphorical accuracy; but Heathcliff is *not* the same. He has not indeed come into a 'sober, disenchanted maturity'—that will be the privilege of Hareton and the second Cathy; but he has completely changed in the fashion that Joseph described much earlier— 'so as by fire'. '... there is a strange change approaching: I'm in its shadow at present', he declares when he has found that nothing is worth the feeling of it. At last, after all the windy tumult and the tempests, he says, 'I have to remind myself to *breathe*...'

If his life, exhausted at the end, has not been, as he once said of it, 'a moral teething', and the novel, therefore, no tragedy, the story of his life has been a moral teething for the author. Lockwood is instructed in the nature of a grand passion, but he and Emily Brontë together are instructed in its final fruits: even roaring fires end in a bed of ashes. Her metaphors instruct her, and her verbs. That besides these rhetorical means (which in their functioning make tolerable the almost impossibly inflated style), she should have found structural means as well which give her whole narrative the remote quality of a twice-told tale, the property of an old wife (and so makes its melodrama endurable), should reinforce the point. At the end, the voice that drones on is the perdurable voice of the country, Nelly Dean's. No more than Heathcliff did Emily Brontë quite intend that homespun finality. Like the older Catherine, Emily Brontë could have said of her book, 'I've dreamed in my life dreams that have stayed with me ever after, and changed my ideas: they've gone through and through me, like wine through water, and altered the colour of my mind'. Her rhetoric altered the form of her intention. It is her education; it shapes her insight.

From 'Fiction and the Matrix of Analogy', *Kenyon Review*, vol. XI, No. 4, 1949, pp. 545 60.

DOROTHY VAN GHENT

The Window Image in *Wuthering Heights*

. . . If the story of Catherine and Heathcliff had not been a story told by an old woman as something that had had its inception many years ago, if the old woman who tells the story had not been limited in imagination and provincial in her sympathies, if the story had been dramatized immediately in the here-and-now and not at a temporal remove and through a dispassioned intermediator, it is doubtful that it would resonate emotionally for us or carry any conviction—even any 'meaning'. Because of the very fact that the impulses it represents are taboo, they can conveniently be observed only at a remove, as someone else's, as of the past, and from the judicial point of view of conventional manners. The 'someone else's' and the 'long ago' are the mind's saving convention for making a distance with itself such as will allow it perspective. Thus the technical *displacement* of Heathcliff's and Catherine's story into past time and into the memory of an old woman functions in the same way as dream displacements: it both censors and indulges, protects and liberates.

Significantly, our first real contact with the Catherine-Heathcliff drama is established through a dream—Lockwood's dream of the ghost-child at the window. Lockwood is motivated to dream the dream by the most easily convincing circumstances; he has fallen asleep while reading Catherine's diary, and during his sleep a tempest-blown branch is scratching on the windowpane. But why should Lockwood, the well-mannered urbanite, dream *this*?

I pulled its wrist on to the broken pane, and rubbed it to and fro till the blood ran down and soaked the bedclothes. . . .

The image is probably the most cruel one in the book. Hareton's hanging puppies, Heathcliff's hanging the springer spaniel, Hindley's forcing a knife between Nelly's teeth or throwing his baby over the staircase, Catherine's leaving the blue print of her nails on Isabella's arm, Heathcliff stamping on Hindley's face—these images and others like them imply savagery or revengefulness or drunkenness or hysteria, but always a motivating set of emotional circumstances. But this is the punctilious Lockwood—whose antecedents and psychology are so insipid that we care little about them—who scrapes the dream-waif's wrist back and forth on broken glass till the blood runs down and soaks the bedclothes. The cruelty of the dream is the gratuitousness of the violence wrought on a child by an emotionally unmotivated vacationer from the city, dreaming in a strange bed. The bed is an old-fashioned closet bed ('a large oak case . . . it formed a little closet' with a window set in it): its panelled sides Lockwood has 'pulled together' before going to sleep. The bed is like a coffin (at the end of the book, Heathcliff dies in it, behind its closed panels); it had been Catherine's bed, and the movable panels themselves suggest the coffin in which she is laid, whose 'panels' Heathcliff bribes the sexton to remove at one side. Psychologically, Lockwood's dream has only the most perfunctory determinations, and nothing at all of result for the dreamer himself, except to put him uncomfortably out of bed. But poetically the dream has its reasons, compacted into the image of the daemonic child scratching at the pane, trying to get from the 'outside' 'in', and of the dreamer in a bed like a coffin, released by that deathly privacy to indiscriminate violence. The coffin-like bed shuts off any interference with the wild deterioration of the psyche. Had the dream used any other agent than the effete, almost epicene Lockwood, it would have lost this symbolic force; for Lockwood, more successfully than anyone else in the book, has shut out the powers of darkness (the pun in his name is obvious in this context); and his lack of any dramatically thorough motivation for dreaming the cruel dream suggests those powers as existing autonomously, not only in the 'outsideness' of external nature, beyond the physical windowpane, but also within, even in the soul least prone to passionate excursion.

The windowpane is the medium, treacherously transparent, separating the 'inside' from the 'outside', the 'human' from the alien and terrible 'other'. Immediately after the incident of the dream, the time of the narrative is displaced into the childhood of Heathcliff and Catherine, and we see the two children looking through the window of the Lintons' drawing room.

> 'Both of us were able to look in by standing on the basement, and clinging to the ledge, and we saw—ah! it was beautiful—a

splendid place carpeted with crimson, and crimson-covered chairs and tables, and a pure white ceiling bordered by gold, a shower of glass-drops hanging in silver chains from the centre, and shimmering with little soft tapers. Old Mr and Mrs Linton were not there; Edgar and his sister had it entirely to themselves. Shouldn't they have been happy? We should have thought ourselves in heaven!'

Here the two unregenerate waifs look *in* from the night on the heavenly vision of the refinements and securities of the most privileged human estate. But Heathcliff rejects the vision: seeing the Linton children blubbering and bored there (*they* cannot get *out!*), he senses the menace of its limitations; while Catherine is fatally tempted. She is taken in by the Lintons, and now it is Heathcliff alone outside looking through the window.

'The curtains were still looped up at one corner, and I resumed my station as a spy; because, if Catherine had wished to return, I intended shattering their great glass panes to a million of fragments, unless they let her out. She sat on the sofa quietly ... the woman-servant brought a basin of warm water, and washed her feet; and Mr Linton mixed a tumbler of negus, and Isabella emptied a plateful of cakes into her lap ... Afterwards, they dried and combed her beautiful hair. ...'

Thus the first snare is laid by which Catherine will be held for a human destiny—her feet washed, cakes and wine for her delectation, her beautiful hair combed (the motifs here are limpid as those of fairy tale, where the changeling in the 'otherworld' is held there mysteriously by bathing and by the strange new food he has been given to eat). By her marriage to Edgar Linton, Catherine yields to that destiny; later she resists it tormentedly and finds her way out of it by death. Literally she 'catches her death' by throwing open the window.

'Open the window again wide: fasten it open! Quick, why don't you move?' [she says to Nelly].
'Because I won't give you your death of cold', I answered.
'You won't give me a chance of life, you mean', she said. ...

In her delirium, she opens the window, leans out into the winter wind, and calls across the moors to Heathcliff,

'Heathcliff, if I dare you now, will you venture? ... Find a way, then! ... You are slow! ... you always followed me!'

On the night after her burial, unable to follow her (though he digs up her grave in order to lie beside her in the coffin from which the side panels have been removed), he returns to the Heights *through the window*—for Hindley has barred the door—to wreak on the living the fury of his frustration. It is years later that Lockwood arrives at the Heights and spends his uncomfortable night there. Lockwood's outcry in his dream brings Heathcliff *to the window*, Heathcliff who has been caught ineluctably in the human to grapple with its interdictions long after Catherine has broken through them. The treachery of the window is that Catherine, lost now in the 'other', can look through the transparent membrane that separates her from humanity, can scratch on the pane, but cannot get 'in', while Heathcliff, though he forces the window open and howls into the night, cannot get 'out'. When he dies, Nelly Dean discovers the window swinging open, the window of that old-fashioned coffin-like bed where Lockwood had had the dream. Rain has been pouring in during the night, drenching the dead man. Nelly says,

> 'I hasped the window; I combed his black long hair from his forehead; I tried to close his eyes: to extinguish, if possible, that frightful, life-like gaze of exultation before any one else beheld it. They would not shut: they seemed to sneer at my attempts. . . .'

Earlier, Heathcliff's eyes have been spoken of as 'the clouded windows of hell' from which a 'fiend' looks out. All the other uses of the 'window' that we have spoken of here are not figurative but perfectly naturalistic uses, though their symbolic value is inescapble. But the fact that Heathcliff's eyes refuse to close in death suggests the symbol in a metaphorical form (the 'fiend' has now got 'out', leaving the window open), elucidating with simplicity the meaning of the 'window' as a separation between the daemonic depths of the soul and the limited and limiting lucidities of consciousness, a separation between the soul's 'otherness' and its humanness. . . .

From *The English Novel: Form and Function*, Harper and Row,
New York and Evanston, 1961, pp. 153-70.

J. F. GOODRIDGE

Nelly as Narrator

. . . Though copious and detailed, Nelly's narrative has an extraordinary sometimes breathless, energy, as if she were describing events that she had witnessed an hour ago, every moment of which is vividly present to her. In this art of stark immediacy—of making the past live for us in the present—we feel that the narrative is moulded by the pressure of events, and not that the shape and interpretation of events is being fashioned by the narrator. The sense of actuality is conveyed by a succession of precise concrete details that fall artlessly into place; and her sureness of touch seems to arise out of an astonishingly clear memory, especially for physical sensations. The impression of rapid excitement is achieved by concentrating our attention on movement and gesture, action and re-action, intermixed with vehement dialogue which convinces by its emphatic speech rhythms and plainness of language:

> 'Oh, if I were but in my own bed in the old house!' she went on bitterly, wringing her hands, 'And that wind sounding in the firs by the lattice. Do let me feel it!—it comes straight down the moor—do let me have one breath!'
> To pacify her, I held the casement ajar a few seconds. A cold blast rushed through; I closed it, and returned to my post. She lay still now, her face bathed in tears. Exhaustion of body had entirely subdued her spirit; our fiery Catherine was no better than a wailing child.

There is no trace here of the conscious stylist. Catherine's words (with their sudden reminder of Lockwood's nightmare) seem to answer perfectly to Wordsworth's conception of poetry distilled to its bare essence—intense feeling overflowing in a naïve directness of language. The words 'it comes straight down the moor' might come from a good ballad or folk-song. (Consider what a difference it would make if we added the word 'from' after 'down', or if 'the' were substituted for the colloquial 'that' in the previous sentence.)

Notice too the brief rapidity of the sentences in the second para-graph; the way the sensation of cold is rendered by the active verb 'rushed'; and the absence of sentimentality in Nelly's diagnosis of Catherine's condition. The servant's familiar contempt for her mis-tress's childish tantrums is tempered by only a touch of motherly concern for her physical illness.

Nelly's value as a narrator is clear from this example. She brings us very close to the action and is, in one way, deeply engaged in it: the intimate affairs of the Heights and the Grange have taken up her whole life. Yet her air of righteous superiority towards Catherine and Heathcliff, her proprietary attitude towards those whom she has nursed as children, prevents her from being too emotionally involved in their affairs. As a professional housekeeper and natural busybody, her con-cern in events is chiefly a practical one, and she represents for us the commonsense point of view. (Suppose that one had to rewrite *Sense and Sensibility* from the point of view of Marianne Dashwood's housekeeper-companion: would she take a harsher view of Marianne than Jane Austen does?) Since Nelly always feels herself called upon to act responsibly, in the best interests (as she imagines) of her master and mistress, she has little time for the luxury of personal feeling.

Though decided in her views, Nelly is sometimes swayed hither and thither by pressures too powerful for her to understand, still less to control, and her own part in them is such as to make the reader doubtful of her judgements. Few readers today can accept her, as Charlotte Brontë did, as a 'specimen of true benevolence and homely fidelity'. Her conventional religious and moral sentiments remind us of normal standards of behaviour, and at the same time are used ironically to stress the inadequacy of those standards and the moral blindness to which they can lead. One of the chief ways in which Brontë controls our responses, is by allowing us to feel we are more perceptive and imaginative than her narrators. . . .

From *Emily Brontë: 'Wuthering Heights'*, Studies in English Literature No. 20, Edward Arnold, London, 1964, pp. 18–20.

[This short book gives a detailed and perceptive analysis of the novel, chapter by chapter.]

MIRIAM ALLOTT

The Rejection of Heathcliff?

. . . Lord David Cecil's main contentions [in *Early Victorian Novelists* (1937)] about the principles of storm and calm and their relationship to each other in the novel are the following. First, they are 'not conflicting': they are to be thought of either as separate aspects of a pervading spirit or as component parts of a harmony. Second, they are not in themselves destructive. . . . Thirdly, the system composed of the balance of these opposites can only be subject to temporary interruptions because it is self-righting. It operates to restore the equilibrium which is momentarily lost. Of the stormy Earnshaws and the Linton 'children of calm', Cecil asserts, 'Together each group, following its own sphere, combines to compose as cosmic harmony. It is the destruction and the re-establishment of this harmony which is the theme of the story.' These are the conclusions drawn by Cecil from his study of the novel, but they are not self-evident conclusions. . . . The conclusions are in themselves extraordinary. If the storm and calm principles are neither conflicting nor destructive, if the discords are only transitory, and if the final harmony is the re-establishment of an original equilibrium, surely *Wuthering Heights* should leave us feeling less troubled and haunted than in fact it does?

Indeed the whole structure of the novel suggests a deeper and more compulsive concern with the elements of 'storm' than this reading allows for. As everyone has noticed, Emily Brontë extends her themes into the story of a second generation of Earnshaws and Lintons; Cecil himself comments on the way in which she uses her two generations to illustrate contrasts between 'calm' and 'storm', and to reveal the workings of inherited characteristics. But he has not seized on what is really significant here. What is most remarkable about the second generation story is the effort it makes to modify the 'storm-calm' opposition in such a way as to eliminate the most violent and troubling elements that give the first generation story its peculiar intensity. Emily Brontë takes great pains in the second part of her story to re-introduce her earlier relationship-patterns and to show them with a new kind of emphasis. She substitutes for the violent Cathy-Edgar-Heathcliff relationships of the first part the milder Catherine-Linton-Hareton relationships of the second; and she alters the earlier savage Hindley-Heathcliff relationship (of victimizer and embittered victim) into the more temperate Heathcliff-Hareton relationship (where the tyrant has some feeling for his victim, while the victim himself remains loving and unembittered). The thoroughness with which she 'works over' the relationships in the earlier parts of her story extends to other situations as well: Hindley's savage and destructive grief for his wife, Frances, and Heathcliff's frenzy at Cathy's death, reappear as Edgar's deep but quiet grief for the same Cathy, and as Hareton's 'strong grief' for Heathcliff—a grief 'which springs naturally from a generous heart, though it be tough as tempered steel'. Again, while Emily Brontë replaces the wildness of the first generation story by a quality of energy in the second generation which is more normal and human, she also shows us in the second generation a demoralizing extreme of calm. Thus Heathcliff, the epitome of 'storm', fathers Linton, who takes 'Linton' qualities, inherited from Isabella, to their furthest point of lethargic inaction.

Seen in this way, the book consciously describes two nearly symmetrical 'arcs'. The first bears us on through the violence of Catherine's and Heathcliff's obsessional feelings for each other, and through the stress of their relationships with the Lintons, to end in a mood of doubtful equipoise (for the spirits, apparently united and at rest, lie near the bare moor, and in the rain and darkness they still 'walk'). The other 'arc', also passing through stress, ends in the quiet of the valley; but the nature of the stress, in this second case, is different, and in accordance with it there is a quieter outcome. The two arcs suggest that the novel is an effort to explore and, *if possible,* to reconcile conflicting 'attractions'; it is sufficiently clear, I think, that Emily Brontë was drawn—though very differently, that is to say by different parts of her nature—towards both storm and calm. In the story of the first generation the clash of these opposites is worked out in terms of a strong emotional commitment to the values of storm. What does such a commitment in all its furthest implications really entail?— this is the question Emily Brontë, with her unsentimental honesty, seems to ask. The answer is troubling. The second part of the novel examines an alternative commitment and poses another question: if storm-values are dangerous or undesirable, what is the nature of the calm that one must try to accept in the place of storm? For example, are we to accept calm if it implies a universe like Linton's, in which men and women are only 'half alive'? The appeal of calm is to the judgment rather than the feelings.

The book's extraordinary power derives at least in part, then, from Emily Brontë's attempt to do justice to the conflicting demands of her heart and head. Her most powerful emotions lie with Heath-cliff (or 'storm', or 'earth in its harsher aspects'—whichever of these labels one prefers). But Heathcliff is ultimately a dark and troubling image to her. . . . It is most unlikely that Emily Brontë found it easy to reconcile the feelings accompanying her 'Heathcliff' passion with other aspects of her personality. She was, after all, simple and devout: and we have plenty of evidence of her piety. . . . Indeed, the second-generation story seems to result from a ruthlessly determined effort to supersede Heathcliff and everything identified with the harsher, more destructive aspects of storm. . . .

I am stressing here that this is the direction in which the second-generation story moves, but of course there is no permanent solution of the conflict in the sense that feeling can be finally defeated by will in the service of intellectual judgment. The rights of feeling are safeguarded in the novel, for Heathcliff, defeated in one way, is triumphant in another. Even though he can no longer prevent the happiness of Hareton Earnshaw and the younger Catherine, he 'retains' the deserted Earnshaw property that he has usurped, inhabiting Wuthering Heights and the bare moorland with the elder Catherine.

At the novel's end a certain equilibrium has been achieved. It is not, however, as Lord David Cecil says, an inevitable harmony follow-ing Heathcliff's posthumous union with his affinity, Catherine, nor the re-establishment of the balance of forces at the beginning of the book when Lintons and Earnshaws existed harmoniously but in separation. It is, in fact, a harmony resulting from a new combination of Earn-shaws and Lintons, with Earnshaw energy modified by Linton calm.

Heathcliff obsessions are excluded. Moreover, in order to achieve the new harmonious alliance, the Earnshaws at last abandon their old house; the significance of this departure is stressed by Emily Brontë's emphasis on the inscription over the old door, which Lockwood notices early in the first chapter—'among a wilderness of crumbling griffins and shameless little boys, I detected the date "1500", and the name "Hareton Earnshaw" '—and which the dispossessed Hareton is so pleased to be able to read for himself in Chapter XXIV. After three hundred years the Earnshaws withdraw from Wuthering Heights and come down to Thrushcross Grange, bringing to the valley some of their own energy but also in their turn being modified by the values it represents. The situation at the end of the novel, therefore, is vastly different from the situation at its beginning.... Perhaps the one clear assertion made by *Wuthering Heights* is that for the purposes of ordinary life—and given the special Earnshaw nature—Lintons are better for Earnshaws than Heathcliff is. To that extent, Emily Brontë's novel makes a moral judgment: but whether her heart goes with the rejection of Heathcliff is another matter.

The interpretation here suggested is, I believe, forced on us by the book's structure, but the evidence from structure may be strengthened by noting the different texture of the writing in different parts of the novel. The emotional quality of the first part of the book is quite different from that of the second, and to a great extent it is the compulsive nature of the imagery in the first-generation story that contributes to this effect. The prevailing images in the first part of the book are sombre and troubling, those of the second part not only carry less disturbing associations, but in many cases they appear to be frankly contrived, though this comment must not lead us into the mistake of thinking them less successful. They are often fresh, vivid and genuinely apt.... The kind of imagery prevailing in each of the two parts expresses the conflict which Emily Brontë heroically attempted to reconcile.

At the last, within the space of a single page, we turn from the phantoms of Heathcliff and the elder Catherine restlessly walking the Heights in rain and thunder ... to contemplate those other 'ramblers' on the moors, Hareton and the younger Catherine, who halt on the threshold of the old house to take 'a last look at the moon—or, more correctly, at each other by her light'. The closing passage of the book might suggest to an unwary reader that the final victory is to them. It is possible to mistake this last comment of Lockwood's, indicating 'calm' after 'storm', for a statement of calm's ultimate triumph. But such a reading overlooks the departure of Hareton and the younger Catherine to the valley, and their abandonment of the old house to the spirits of the still restless Heathcliff and the elder

Catherine. There is, after all, no escape for Emily Brontë from her emotional commitment to Heathcliff; there can only be an intellectual judgment that for the purposes of ordinary life he will not do. It is the artist's business, Tchekov tells us, to set questions, not solve them, and Emily Brontë sets her very personal question in terms that establish the greatness of her art. It is less a sign of any flaw in her achievement than an indication of the urgency of her internal conflict that the tones of her own voice can be heard even through her admirably controlled 'oblique and indirect view' of Catherine's and Heathcliff's fated alliance. The tones are those of someone aware that the claims of head and heart remain unreconciled.

From *Essays in Criticism*, vol. VIII, No. 1, 1958, pp. 27–47.

BORIS FORD

An Analysis of *Wuthering Heights*

...*Wuthering Heights*... is not an unpleasant novel, and one of the main purposes of this analysis will be to demonstrate that it is in fact a very precisely balanced structure of 'pleasant' and 'unpleasant', 'normal' and 'abnormal'. Far from giving way to melodrama and self-indulgence, Emily Brontë relegates all the potentially unhealthy elements to their place in the artistic whole, and the novel moves continually towards a resolution of perfect tranquillity. At the centre of *Wuthering Heights* lies, of course, the relationship between Cathy and Heathcliff;[1] for the second half of the book there is a closely allied theme, the relationship between Catherine and Hareton, the latter theme acting, in its similarity to the former, as a commentary, though upon a very different emotional plane.[2] There are in addition several subsidiary themes which serve to determine and qualify the attitude to be adopted by the reader. The novel is almost entirely recounted by two observers, Mrs Dean and Lockwood, for much the greater part by the former. Lockwood, in fact, has no more than the first and the last words, and for the rest he merely listens to Mrs Dean's story as a representative of a world foreign to the events that take place. As such he tends to be both uncomprehending and insensi-

[1] For the sake of clarity I refer throughout to Catherine Earnshaw, with whom Heathcliff is in love, as 'Cathy', and to her daughter, Catherine Linton, as 'Catherine'.
[2] The reader is referred here to the family tree of the Earnshaws, Lintons and Heathcliffs worked out by C. P. Sanger. See p. 55 of the present volume.

tive; he explains, for instance, that his search for solitude is to help him forget an unsuccessful love-affair:

> While enjoying a month of fine weather at the sea-coast, I was thrown into the company of a most fascinating creature: a real goddess in my eyes, as long as she took no notice of me. I 'never told my love' vocally; still, if looks have language, the merest idiot might have guessed I was head over ears . . .

The vulgarity of this is enforced by the flat and lifeless prose; and the absurdity of Lockwood's passion helps to bring out by contrast the significance of the Cathy-Heathcliff relationship. Lockwood's response, at subsequent points in the novel, is more or less what the response of the ordinary reader might be expected to be. At first unsympathetic, he is by the end entirely reconciled to all that has taken place. He has not long made the acquaintance of Heathcliff and Wuthering Heights before he feels that

> The dismal spiritual atmosphere of the place overcame, and more than neutralized the glowing physical comforts around me; and I resolved to be cautious how I ventured under the rafters a third time.

Having thus recorded the natural reaction of an observer as yet unacquainted with the deeper cross-currents of emotion, Lockwood tends to suspend judgment until the end of the novel.

Mrs Dean's function in the novel cannot be so simply stated; she may be said to act as Chorus with the difference that she offers a point of view which is not altogether disinterested. As raconteuse she naturally has to move upon a plane of normal and sometimes trivial consciousness that excludes her to some extent from the emotional atmosphere of the Cathy-Heathcliff relationship; but this apart, she represents the maximum objectivity possible to any active participant in the events described. Her essential qualifications appear when Lockwood says to her:

> 'Excepting a few provincialisms of slight consequence, you have no marks of the manners which I am habituated to consider peculiar to your class. I am sure you have thought a great deal more than the generality of servants think. You have been compelled to cultivate your reflective faculties for want of occasions for frittering away your life in silly trifles.'

Mrs Dean laughed.

> 'I certainly esteem myself a steady, reasonable kind of body', she said; 'not exactly from living among the hills and seeing one set of faces, and one series of actions, from year's end to year's end;

but I have undergone sharp discipline, which has taught me wisdom: and then, I have read more than you would fancy, Mr Lockwood. You could not open a book in this library that I have not looked into, and got something out of also ...'

The key-words—'think', 'reflective faculties', 'steady', 'reasonable', 'sharp discipline', 'wisdom'—emphasize the essential normality, the spiritual poise which informs the whole novel. And it is important that Mrs Dean's 'wisdom' is not an exclusively rural heritage, and comes 'not exactly from living among the hills'; it is also derived from a wide reading, and it is this which endows her with a width and generosity of opinion that contrast very strongly with the narrow calvinism of old Joseph, who says to Heathcliff:

'Aw hed aimed tuh dee, where Aw'd sarved fur sixty year ...'

If Lockwood is not to be trusted as a commentator, he being almost a foreigner, nor is Joseph, who is too exclusively part of the environment to offer any semblance of impartiality.

The central theme, as has been suggested, is the relationship between Cathy and Heathcliff. Emily Brontë, however, has no particular concern with the surface appearance of this relationship, but insists throughout on its inner tension. To Mrs Dean, Cathy is explicit:

'This is for the sake of one [Heathcliff] who comprehends in his person my feelings to Edgar [Cathy's future husband] and myself. I cannot express it; but surely you and everybody have a notion that there is or should be an existence beyond you. What were the use of my creation if I were entirely contained here? My great miseries in this world have been Heathcliff's miseries; and I have watched and felt each from the beginning: my great thought in living is himself. If all else perished, and he remained, I should still continue to be; and if all else remained, and he were annihilated, the universe would turn to a mighty stranger: I should not seem a part of it. My love for Linton is like the foliage in the woods: time will change it, I'm well aware, as winter changes the trees. My love for Heathcliff resembles the eternal rocks beneath: a source of little visible delight, but necessary. Nelly, I *am* Heathcliff. He's always, always in my mind: not as a pleasure, any more than I am always a pleasure to myself, but as my own being. So don't talk of our separation again: it is impracticable ...'

Elsewhere she says:

'Whatever our souls are made of, his and mine are the same.'

And Heathcliff, speaking of the dead Cathy, says:

'I *cannot* live without my life! I *cannot* live without my soul!'

Though the point should not be much laboured, there exists a distinct similarity between these passages and the one by Charlotte describing Emily's enforced absence from Haworth; and the comparison serves to emphasize the non-personal nature of the Cathy-Heathcliff relationship.

The key-sentence in the first passage quoted is 'My love for Heathcliff resembles the eternal rocks beneath'. This imagery drawn from nature, and particularly from its sterner elements, is recurrent in the descriptions of Heathcliff. Mrs Dean describes him as being 'hard as whinstone', and when he and the refined Edgar appear together, she says that 'The contrast resembled what you see in exchanging a bleak, hilly, coal country for a beautiful fertile valley'. Cathy is even more outspoken, and describes him as 'an arid wilderness of furze and whinstone'. But, in contrast with the 'red eyes and the fearful blackened inflation of the lineaments' of Mrs Rochester, Heathcliff is presented as being physically quite attractive. Lockwood finds that 'he has an erect and handsome figure', and Mrs Dean says that 'his manner was even dignified: quite divested of roughness, though too stern for grace'. In so far as Heathcliff is abnormal, if that is the right word, it is an abnormality that tends to lie below the level of social deportment. Cathy says:

'Pray don't imagine that he conceals depths of benevolence and affection beneath a stern exterior! He's not a rough diamond —a pearl-containing oyster of a rustic: he's a fierce, pitiless, wolfish man.'

Heathcliff relates how he has 'taught him [his son] to scorn everything extra-animal as silly and weak'; and later he says: 'It's odd what a savage feeling I have to anything that seems afraid of me.' And finally Isabella, his wife, contributes to the impression of the non-human element in Heathcliff, when she asks: 'Is Mr Heathcliff a man? If so, is he mad? And if not, is he a devil?'

With the death of Cathy, however, what was once latent now emerges, and Heathcliff ceases to be dignified. Mrs Dean relates how, just before her death, he 'foamed like a mad dog'; and he himself says: 'You know, I was wild after she died.' The balanced relationship is now broken up, and a great contrast is evident between Cathy and Heathcliff. Mrs Dean says of the former:

... hers [was the hush] of perfect peace. Her brow smooth, her lids closed, her lips wearing the expression of a smile; no angel

in heaven could be more beautiful than she appeared. And I
partook of the infinite calm in which she lay; my mind was never
in a holier frame than while I gazed on that untroubled image of
Divine rest... To be sure, one might have doubted, after the
wayward and impatient existence she had led, whether she
merited a haven of peace at last. One might doubt in seasons of
cold reflection; but not then, in the presence of her corpse. It
asserted its own tranquillity.'

As for Heathcliff, Mrs Dean finds him 'leant against an old ash tree.'
After talking to him, she relates:

'He dashed his head against the knotted trunk; and, lifting up
his eyes, howled, not like a man, but like a savage beast getting
goaded to death with knives and spears.'

The contrast is not only one of verbal description, but also of movement; the Cathy passage runs very smoothly and evenly, and reflects
the 'tranquillity'; whereas the Heathcliff passage is lumpy and awkward to read, generally uneasy in motion. The contrast persists, by
implication, till the end of the novel. Heathcliff's behaviour remains
weird and unnatural. He now bends all his energies towards bringing
under one control the two properties of Wuthering Heights, where he
has lived, and Thrushcross Grange, where Cathy lived with her husband, Edgar Linton. This undertaking, symbolizing his desire to be
re-united with Cathy, obsesses him, and he lets nothing stand in his
way. He shows, for instance, considerable subtlety and brutality in
arranging the marriage between Linton, his son, and Catherine, to
whom Thrushcross Grange will belong on the death of Edgar. The
essential clue to his behaviour is supplied by Catherine, who says to
him:

'Mr Heathcliff, you have nobody to love you; and, however miserable you make us, we still have the revenge of thinking that your
cruelty arises from your greater misery!'

But, once the mundane union has been effected, Heathcliff subsides.
He goes and looks at Cathy in her coffin—'I saw her face again—
it is hers yet'—and says to Mrs Dean:

'She [Cathy] has disturbed me, night and day through eighteen
years—incessantly—remorsely—till yesternight; and yesternight
I was tranquil. I dreamt I was sleeping the last sleep by that
sleeper, with my heart stopped and my cheek frozen against
hers.'

He now has 'a single wish', and his 'whole being and faculties are
yearning to attain it'. The ordinary physical demands of life have no

more interest for him: 'I have to remind myself to breathe—almost to remind my heart to beat!' He moves nearer and nearer towards the unspecified goal; 'I'm too happy, and yet I'm not happy enough. My soul's bliss kills my body, but does not satisfy itself.' And finally Mrs Dean relates:

> 'Mr Heathcliff was there—laid on his back. His eyes met mine so keen and fierce, I started; and then he seemed to smile . . . he was dead and stark!'

He is buried, as he had demanded, with Cathy; and the final cadence comes with the small boy's story:

> 'They's Heathcliff, and a woman, yonder under t'Nab,' he blubbered, 'un' Aw darnut pass 'em'.

The level on which the Cathy-Heathcliff relationship has moved, and its depersonalized character, make it seem entirely fitting that it should attain equilibrium and tranquillity only with the death of the two persons concerned.

The structure of *Wuthering Heights,* as has been shown by C. P. S. in a Hogarth pamphlet, is truly remarkable for the degree to which it seems to have been artificially constructed, with minute attention paid to details of apparent irrelevance.[1] Analysis reveals, however, that this is not a symptom of misapplied energy and interest in Emily Brontë, but is precisely what gives the novel its coherence. The stresses and contradictions inherent in the Cathy-Heathcliff theme just analysed are reflected in varying ways in all the relationships of the novel; heredity, above all, plays a structural and unifying rôle that merits some attention at this point. The fundamental conflict emerges in the contrast between the two estates, between Thrushcross Grange —'a splendid place carpeted with crimson, and crimson covered chairs and tables', and Wuthering Heights—'the floor was of smooth white stones; the chairs high-backed, primitive structures, painted green'. Thrushcross Grange is the home of the Lintons, and Edgar

---

[1] The general theory, of course, is that *Wuthering Heights* is put together in a singularly shoddy manner. H. W. Garrod, in his Introduction to the Oxford Edition (this Introduction is probably one of the most sympathetic and well-meaning pieces of writing on the novel), finds that:

> The faults of *Wuthering Heights* proceed, not from defective knowledge of human nature, but from inferior technique, from an insufficient acquaintance with the craft of fiction.

Other critics have favoured the theory that the novel is by two people, Bramwell writing the first part. This absurdity has been convincingly refuted by Miss Irene Cooper Willis, whose pamphlet, *The Authorship of Wuthering Heights,* published by the Hogarth Press, contains some excellent close analysis of the texture of the prose.

and Isabella Linton, together with Frances, stand for refinement and delicacy. In contrast there are Hindley and Cathy Earnshaw and Heathcliff, all of whom were brought up in Wuthering Heights, and develop very roughly and without the civilized graces. In comparison with the 'beautiful fertile valley' of Edgar, Heathcliff is a 'bleak, hilly coal country'. As a girl Cathy was a 'wild, wicked slip', but, after staying for some time with the Lintons, she returns 'a very dignified person'; the Linton environment tends to eradicate from her the wilder elements that remain in Heathcliff. There are two inter-marriages: Heathcliff marries Isabella, and Cathy marries Edgar. The former marriage is a complete failure; Heathcliff shatters Isabella, and their son, Linton, is utterly spineless and wastes away rapidly. The second marriage is more successful; Mrs Dean believes that Cathy and Edgar 'were really in possession of deep and growing happiness'. Their daughter is Catherine, of whom Mrs Dean says:

> 'Her spirit was high, though not rough, and qualified by a heart sensitive and lively to excess in its affections. That capacity for intense attachments reminded me of her mother: still she did not resemble her; for she could be as soft and mild as a doe, and she had gentle voice and pensive expression: her anger was never furious: her love never fierce; it was deep and tender.'

The implications of these marriages and their offspring are fairly general. The first emphasizes the incompatibility of the Heathcliff and Isabella elements. And the second reveals that there exists a potential sympathy between the two conflicting houses; Cathy, her nature modified by a stay at Thrushcross Grange, marries Edgar with comparative success, and their daughter meets with as great approval as Heathcliff's son with contempt from Mrs Dean. And finally there is Hareton, the son of Frances and Hindley, Cathy's brother. Up till the age of about seventeen, Hareton is almost a replica of Heathcliff, though the Frances influence renders him more subdued, she being an insignificant and frail person. Mrs Dean says that Heath-cliff 'appeared to have bent his malevolence on making him [Hareton] a brute'; and not long before Heathcliff dies, he says:

> 'Hareton seemed a personification of my youth, not a human being . . . his startling likeness to Catherine [Cathy] connected him fearfully with her . . . Hareton's aspect was the ghost of my immortal love, of my wild endeavours to hold my right, my degradation, my pride, my happiness, and my anguish . . .'

The differences between the two main themes, Cathy-Heathcliff and Catherine-Hareton, lie, very generally, in the fact that the former is wilder and more Lawrentian. For instance, Cathy and Heathcliff do not marry; Cathy tells Mrs Dean that their relationship has no need for sanctions of that kind, and that it is not likely to be affected by her marriage to Edgar. And the same applies to Heathcliff's marriage to Isabella, Edgar's sister. In fact the Cathy-Heathcliff relationship is handled in neither sexual nor even particularly human terms. On the other hand, the Catherine-Hareton theme moves on a plane of normal procedure; at the end of the novel they are about to be married. And this distinction between the two themes is of fundamental importance: the Catherine-Hareton relationship is the projection into the sphere of ordinary behaviour of the Cathy-Heathcliff relationship; it is the expression in conventional social terms of the main spiritual conflict. As in the description of Catherine quoted above, on the one hand the anger is 'furious' and the love 'fierce', on the other everything is 'soft and mild', 'gentle', and 'pensive'.

Between Catherine and Hareton, however, there is no such immediate sympathy as there was between Cathy and Heathcliff. The former relationship being, as has been suggested, a counterpart of the latter, it develops from outside itself. Cathy dies in giving birth to Catherine, and so, just as from this moment she and Heathcliff are separated and only very slowly re-united, similarly there exists from the first a lack of sympathy between Catherine and Hareton which is only gradually overcome. At their first meeting she mistakes him for a servant, and he retorts:

'I'll see thee damned before I be *thy* servant.'

Heathcliff's struggle to unite the two estates involves marrying his son, Linton, to Catherine, and this naturally throws her further apart from Hareton. But, once the marriage has taken place (Linton dies almost immediately) and Heathcliff feels himself moving ever closer to Cathy, intimacy between Catherine and Hareton springs up rapidly. And, significantly linking up with Mrs Dean's remarks about her literary education, it is in teaching Hareton to read and appreciate her books that Catherine gives impetus to this relationship. Mrs Dean says:

'His honest, warm, and intelligent nature shook off rapidly the clouds of ignorance and degradation in which it had been bred; and Catherine's sincere commendations acted as a spur to his industry.'

It is this relationship which meets with Mrs Dean's approval. Her comments on Heathcliff and Cathy are fundamentally sympathetic, but none the less qualified. After Cathy has told her of her feelings for Heathcliff—'Nelly, I *am* Heathcliff!—she says that she 'was out of patience with her folly!'; and after Cathy's death she says:

'Retracing the course of Catherine Linton, I fear we have no right to think she is [happy in the other world]; but we'll leave her with her Maker.'

And when she finds Heathcliff in the grounds, and sees him dash 'his head against the knotted trunk', she observes that 'It hardly moved my compassion'. But of Hareton and Catherine she says:

'The crown of all my wishes will be the union between these two. I shall envy no one on their wedding-day: there won't be a happier woman than myself in England!'

But the 'union between these two' symbolizes also the final union of Cathy and Heathcliff. The close sympathy between the two themes now emerges clearly. When Heathcliff dies, Hareton 'sat by the corpse all night, weeping in bitter earnest'. The resolution into tranquillity with which the Cathy-Heathcliff theme ends is paralleled in the Hareton-Catherine theme. As Mrs Dean tells Lockwood that the latter are going to live at Thrushcross Grange, they return from a walk.

'They are afraid of nothing', I [Lockwood] grumbled, watching their approach through the window. 'Together, they would brave satan and all his legions.'
As they stepped onto the door-stones, and halted to take a last look at the moon—or, more correctly, at each other, by her light— I felt irresistibly impelled to escape them . . .

Lockwood, whose sympathies are now fully engaged, goes to find the graves of Edgar, Cathy and Heathcliff.

I lingered round them, under the benign sky: watched the moths fluttering among the heather and hare-bells; listened to the soft wind breathing through the grass; and wondered how anyone could ever imagine unquiet slumbers for the sleepers in that quiet earth.

The even and balanced movement of the prose, and the particularity of the description, bring the novel to a close on a note of great calm and completeness. . . .

From an article by Boris Ford in *Scrutiny*, vol. VII, No. 4, 1939, pp. 375–89.

VINCENT BUCKLEY

Passion and Control in *Wuthering Heights*

... The book depends, both for its quality of self-subsistent realism and its presentation of high passion, on the quality of the chief speeches. Almost without exception, these are speeches made by Catherine or Heathcliff; and they establish both a similarity and a dissimilarity with Shakespearean tragedy. In both Shakespeare and Brontë the chief speeches organize the narrative *poetically*, though in very different ways. For example, Shakespeare uses the great speeches of Lear or Cleopatra to concentrate his narrative, so that the whole play seems to press in on them and take fire from them. Brontë is writing prose fiction, and at much greater length than any Shakespearean tragedy; she is having the events narrated at second, or third, or fourth hand, not presented on stage; and the great speeches of *Wuthering Heights* therefore have a somewhat different effect; they do not concentrate everything else in themselves, but spread their power gradually and unobtrusively through all the other events, like a clear note through the night air or (to use Brontë's own term) like wine through water.

There are two things, I think, which accomplish this fusion of seemingly disparate elements. One is the quality of the vision embodied in the central relationship between Catherine and Heathcliff, and represented in their chief speeches; the other is the quality of the book's staple language, which invites us to speak of 'vision' in a more inclusive sense. ...

It does seem to me that the staple prose of the book is remotely energized by the imaginative force of the great speeches; but, of course, its nature is different: less lyrical, passionate, declaratory. It is, in fact, a markedly unexcited prose, leisurely, explanatory, called forth in the narrators' effort at the recreation of events which, being so extraordinary, need a more than usual restraint to establish their veracity. Yet it is neither dull nor uniform; within the novel's chosen narrative terms, it has great variety, many weaknesses, a recurrent and flexible strength. For one thing, while its pace and tone show us Lockwood and Nelly Dean as it were determining the language itself, and to some degree giving it its controlled strength, there are many moments which show us Emily Brontë using certain habits of language to present, control, and place the narrators in their turn.

Perhaps 'control' is a misleading word. Actually, it is a process of mutual heightening and definition, such as we find in the greatest dramatic writers. And it reminds us that the novel is no mere hymn to adolescent passion, and no mere tract against hatred and revenge, but a story deliberately fashioned and controlled to the point where the highly individual emotions which its author brings to it are objectified and even universalized. . . .

We can see the staple qualities of the prose in the opening pages, which in so short a space do so much: they present an extraordinary situation which demands to be explained, they characterize and place Lockwood as a person quite unlikely to understand whatever explanation is given, and they suggest a world which, whatever emotions dominate it, is solidly real:

> 'Thrushcross Grange is my own, sir', he interrupted, wincing, 'I should not allow any one to inconvenience me, if I could hinder it—walk in!'
> The 'walk in' was uttered with closed teeth, and expressed the sentiment, 'Go to the Deuce': even the gate over which he leaned manifested no sympathizing movement to the words; and I think that circumstance determined me to accept the invitation: I felt interested in a man who seemed more exaggeratedly reserved than myself.[1]

Look at the way that word 'sympathizing' is used: it emphasizes Lockwood's complacement but earnest insensitivity, establishes his ponderous wit, so out of touch with what Wuthering Heights represents, and shows us a narrator self-preening, faintly absurd, but shrewd and not unmanly. . . . If we jump forward a few chapters, into the heart-beat of the narrative, we find the process advanced:

> Heathcliff lifted his hand, and the speaker sprang to a safer distance, obviously acquainted with its weight. Having no desire to be entertained by a cat-and-dog combat, I stepped forward briskly, as if eager to partake the warmth of the hearth, and innocent of any knowledge of the interrupted dispute. Each had enough decorum to suspend further hostilities: Heathcliff placed his fists, out of temptation, in his pockets; Mrs Heathcliff curled her lip, and walked to a seat far off, where she kept her word by playing the part of a statue during the remainder of my stay. That was not long. I declined joining their breakfast, and, at the first gleam of dawn, took an opportunity of escaping into the free air, now clear and still, and cold as impalpable ice. (Chap. III, p. 36)

---

[1] *Wuthering Heights*, World Classics, 1950, Chap. I, p.1. Page numbers of further quotations are given in the text, and refer to this edition.

We have recorded here a scene which contains the possibility, even the threat, of violence: but the prose itself is not overwhelmed by the violence it presents. We may be momentarily disturbed by 'curled her lip'; but for the most part, it is a careful, slow-moving, even slightly pedantic prose. Emily Brontë is obviously not trying to give anyone, even herself, an emotional *frisson,* but to use her prose to isolate and define human gestures in such a way as to suggest the attitudes behind them. The slowness, the deliberate quality of the prose are necessary for this; they enable her to isolate the important gestures from one another and, by isolating them, to suggest at once the personalities of the people who make them and the presence in the situation of a violence which is never far beneath the surface. This violence gives a peculiar emotional charge to every action but never becomes melodrama. 'Cold as impalpable ice', though it indicates an unusually heightened sensuous response, is the phrase of a writer more interested in a manifold reality than in 'self-expression'.

We notice, too, that this first of the great scenes falls away, as so many others do, into carefully composed descriptions which remind us that the milieu whose solid actuality is to be established is not only, or primarily, a human one (and certainly not, in any ordinary sense, a 'social' one) but one dominated by natural forces, now quiescent, but daunting:

> My landlord hallooed for me to stop, . . . the windings of the road. (Chap. III, pp. 36–37) [*Please find the passage and read it through*]

The emotional intensity, then, is created partly by a prose which refuses to inflate it. Yet that singular combination cannot really be seen at the length of a paragraph; it is a matter not merely of how one particular event or confrontation is defined but of the transitions from perspective to perspective which, as I suggested before, enable Brontë's vision to be so inclusive. To see it more adequately, one would have to take a passage, of considerable length, where we find the raconteur's prose rising by controlled stages to some great speech or speeches, and then, by the way in which it declines from such a peak, both placing and enhancing the speech. It is obvious that, at certain points, the pressure of Brontë's insights and of her characters' (and her own) emotions comes to an almost frightening pitch; and it is at such points that one may immediately test in what ways the book fuses qualities of the conventional novel with those of poetic drama. I think inevitably of the section beginning in the middle of Chapter IX and continuing through Chapter X: from the account of Catherine's decision to marry Edgar Linton to Heathcliff's return from some mysterious school for the civilizing of barbarians ready to overthrow the Linton household.

This passage has a climactic effect; and it covers the passing of several crucial years; yet it is presented with an extraordinary brevity and economy which make one think immediately of the late plays of Shakespeare. Brontë is completely free from the vice of the 'realistic' novelist, the tendency to let the spiritual drama of her characters half-drown in a lake of background detail. Her treatment of time passing, of spiritual cause and effect, while it suggests an intense awareness of growth and loss, has also a remarkable confidence and surety very like those exhibited by Shakespeare in *The Winter's Tale* or *King Lear*. The fateful decision is made, the lovers part in a torment of mutual misunderstanding; and then it is off-stage that all those other decisions and commitments are made which bring them together again, ready to play out their dark destinies, but with personalities significantly changed because they are charged with habits and attitudes built up during the years of isolation.

The account of these episodes has other qualities, too, which heighten the poetic-dramatic vision while rendering it with a certain commonsense realism. For example, although Catherine's passionate nature is amply expressed in what Emily Brontë presents of her speech and gestures, that nature is implicitly criticized as well as expressed. Here the importance of Nelly Dean as narrator is seen; it is through *her* account that Emily Brontë presents Catherine in a realistic, unillusioned way, without sentimentality or glamour. She scowls, frowns, speaks with irritation and hauteur, hectors Nelly, and so on. And yet, in the middle of this extraordinarily tough-minded dialogue comes the great central affirmation of her feeling for Heathcliff; into the keen observations and realistic assessments of the novelist comes the power of the exalted lyrical poet:

'Oh! don't, Miss Catherine!' I cried. '. . . and Linton's is as different as a moonbeam from lightning, or frost from fire.' (Chap. IX, pp. 96–97) [*Please find the passage and read it through*]

The rhythm of this is superb. Not only does Emily Brontë's control of the situation enable her to pass without any strain from an implicit criticism of Catherine to a virtual identification with her; it also enables her to lead gradually from a conversation which, after all, has something soberly conventional about it to one which is piercing in its intensity. The unillusioned reticence of the dialogue form prepares us for the lyrical declaration; for the slow mounting of intensity in the exchanges is also a mounting of intensity in Catherine's emotion. Yet the slowness, the control, prevent her declaration, when it comes, from seeming melodramatic. It is to be accepted as naturally as we

accept one of Lear's speeches on the heath. And there is more to
come: after two more pages of dialogue comes a still more fervent
declaration:

'It is not', retorted she; 'it is the best! The others were the
satisfaction of my whims: and for Edgar's sake, too, to satisfy
him. This is for the sake of one who comprehends in his person
my feelings to Edgar and myself. I cannot express it; but surely
you and everybody have a notion that there is or should be an
existence of yours beyond you. What were the use of my creation,
if I were entirely contained here? My great miseries in this
world have been Heathcliff's miseries, and I watched and felt
each from the beginning: my great thought in living is himself.
If all else perished, and *he* remained, *I* should still continue to
be; and if all else remained, and he were annihilated, the universe
would turn to a mighty stranger: I should not seem a part of
it. My love for Linton is like the foliage in the woods: time will
change it, I'm well aware, as winter changes the trees. My love
for Heathcliff resembles the eternal rocks beneath: a source of
little visible delight, but necessary. Nelly, I *am* Heathcliff! He's
always, always in my mind: not as a pleasure, any more than
I am always a pleasure to myself, but as my own being. So
don't talk of our separation again: it is impracticable; and—'
She paused, and hid her face in the folds of my gown; but I
jerked it forcibly away. I was out of patience with her folly!
(Chap. IX, pp. 99–100)

This speech too is built up on a series of rhythmic movements which
are compelling in their force. They have something breathless about
them, yet they are linked quite logically, so that, while the rhythmic
surge communicates emotion, the actual language has an odd restraint,
even a formality which comes from the finely placed qualifying clauses.
Catherine is not merely expressing an emotion, she is struggling to
define it; and Emily Brontë, by making Nelly Dean the recipient of
it, uses it to continue the definition of Catherine's personality which
has been going on throughout the scene. . . .

[The book] does not use the rhythms and language of prose-poetry
to decorate or glamourize the action; on the contrary, it uses them
to bring out a dimension of the action which the usual methods of
the 'realistic' novelist could not even reach. At the same time, it
leads us to this dimension of experience by building on the sort of
keen unillusioned observation of speech, gesture and personality which
all good novelists have. If *Wuthering Heights* is a 'poetic novel', the
stress must fall equally on the adjective and the noun: on the 'novel'
as fully as on the 'poetic'. And the prose is controlled not just at the

level of individual scenes and paragraphs but in a more expansive way; Brontë's objectifying energy is characteristic rather than intermittent. . . .

It is not just at the scale of the separate paragraph that control is exercised; the tonal variety is seen in the nature of the transitions from one perspective to another, so that passages in themselves uncontrolled or even melodramatic are led to contribute to a much more complex vision. The prose does not precisely subdue the drama of the events or the intensity of the emotional life; if it did, Heathcliff and Catherine would not be the presences we feel them to be; rather, it creates the drama of the events and the intensity of the emotions. But, at the same time, it places them, regulates them, perhaps even criticizes them: in fact, it is by doing so that it creates them so credibly.

It does so partly by the sheer pace, the economy with which transitions are made from one event to another, and from one aspect of the tragedy to another. We are constantly being reminded by such matters that Nelly Dean does not consider herself emotionally, but only morally involved; and we are reminded of this by the pace of the transitions perhaps more than by anything else. But these qualities of the prose are important for other reasons besides their capacity to further define Nelly Dean's role. I think we may say that the slow, careful articulation of each event combined with the pace of the transition from one event or angle of interest to another actually presents, establishes, defines the passion which the book exists to present and define, and which, in fact, permeates it. It is Brontë's quite remarkably original *restraint* which creates the intensity: so that the creative intensity is not a matter of a few isolated intense moments but is communicated to and through the whole book. The next chapter, XVII, opens in a most interesting way:

That Friday made the last of our fine days, for a month. . . .
My anger was greater than my astonishment for a minute.
(Chap. XVII, p. 209) [*Please find the passage and read it through*]

The human storms having been temporarily played to an end by the sheer quality of the prose, with its springtime atmosphere, the natural storms come. The implication is both clear and unobtrusive: Catherine's laying to rest unleashes the restless powers of nature, in a presage of the human storms which are later to vibrate through the affairs of the second generation. The association of human and cosmic powers could hardly be more evident; but though evident, it is, as I say, paradoxical. . . .

The Love between Catherine and Heathcliff

I think it is necessary ... to ask what, so to speak, is the *content* of that passion [between Catherine and Heathcliff], what is its basis and the direction of its development. What characterizes it is not just its intensity or its duration, not just the amazing sense of two lives harmonized at an unusual depth, either, but also the appalling inner twists and thwartings of each of the personalities—particularly, of course, Heathcliff's—which seem to come not only from their being parted but also from the strain which the love itself suffers from having to live in a world that simply will not accommodate it....

Certainly, the sense of harmony, most profound and rare psychic harmony, which the love rests on is the first obvious fact about it:

> 'My love for Heathcliff resembles the eternal rocks beneath: a source of little visible delight, but necessary. Nelly, I *am* Heathcliff! He's always, always in my mind: not as a pleasure, any more than I am always a pleasure to myself, but as my own being. So don't talk of our separation again—it is impracticable;'

That is the first view which Catherine declares; and when Heathcliff returns to find her 'happily' married to Edgar Linton, she confesses to Nelly that his coming has reconciled her to the universe:

> 'The event of this evening has reconciled me to God ... Goodnight! I'm an angel!' (Chap. X, p. 122) [*Please find the passage and read it through*]

The religious tone here is slightly different from that which dominates the earlier, more vibrant passage; and, while Catherine's stress is still on the psychic harmony which is the very basis and character of her love for Heathcliff, the stress now falls less fiercely. It is, in fact, placed more on the feeling of being reconciled by Heathcliff's presence with God and humanity; so, while it is less vibrant, it is more obviously humane, perhaps more ordinary, in nature.

This feeling does not remain for very long in its pure state. Between Heathcliff's return and Catherine's death she and we have had many proofs of his brutality, which make it clear that, however reconciled to the universe she is through *him,* he is not at all reconciled to it through *her.* The difference between their two attitudes is nowhere more extreme, and nowhere, I suggest, more puzzling. The difference, or loss of understanding, breaks out into quarrelling:

> 'I seek no revenge on you', replied Heathcliff ... 'the most efficient method of revenging yourself on me.' (Chap. XI, pp. 138-9) [*Please find the passage and read it through*]

What has happened, now, to Catherine's earlier feeling of having been reconciled with 'God and humanity'? What we are presented with now is an image of something not very far from mutual and compulsive parasitism. And we should note, too, that when Catherine is dying, not many pages further on, and there *is* some kind of reconciliation, it is full of reproaches, so violent as to appear quite ambivalent, offering more torment than spiritual satisfaction. The whole centre of chapter XV records the fluctuations of their emotions; and an unusually passionate exchange culminates in Catherine's declaration:

> 'Oh, you see, Nelly, he would not relent a moment. . . . Heathcliff, dear! you should not be sullen now. Do come to me, Heathcliff.' (Chap. XV, p. 198) [*Please find the passage and read it through*]

This is the last of Catherine's great speeches. . . . What I want to point to is Catherine's apparent recognition of the virtual impossibility of their love as a relationship to be realized on earth. This speech is, of course, the speech of a distracted and dying woman; yet I think it significant that it is so different in its spiritual and emotional emphases from the much earlier speech ('I *am* Heathcliff') There throbs in it, I think, a recognition of strain, limitations, even impossibility, which was joyously absent from the earlier one. . . . I almost feel that the pain which [the love] causes both the lovers is not circumstantial but is intrinsic to the nature of the love as something requiring realization *in an actual world*.

What, then, is the nature of that love? The question is almost unanswerable. One critic declares confidently that it has nothing sexual about it, that it is just an extremely intense form of friendship. This seems to me nonsense. The relationship vibrates at every point with sexual suggestion. For example, immediately after the passage I last quoted occurs the following paragraph:

> In her eagerness she rose and supported herself on the arm . . . and held my tongue, in great perplexity. (Chap. XVI, pp. 198–9) [*Please find the passage and read it through*]

Again, as so often, the melodrama of the passage comes not so much from the lovers' actions as from Nelly's perceptions of them ('foamed like a mad dog'). But the passion recorded here is surely sexual in character: we might almost say, sexual not in its overt expression but at root, at depth.

At root sexual, and in an odd, perhaps Lawrentian sense, religious as well. I use the word with a conscious sense of its paradox, and in no desire to introduce 'transcendent realities' which the author herself has not introduced. This is by no means a devotional or theological work; yet 'religious' seems to me precisely the right word. It is perhaps misleading to use the word 'adolescent' at all in characterizing the relationship; for, whereas it has an intensity and an inwardness which may be familiar to some people from adolescence, its basis, its nature, is one which I should be surprised to find that adolescence had familiarized us with.

The nature of that relationship is, then, as important as its intensity. And the nature of the relationship is one of an extraordinary psychic harmony seen, first, as a fact, later, as a recovered possibility, and, last, as an impossibility in any earthly terms. Are we to think of the love, then, as being consummated in heaven? ... We must, after all, take with great seriousness Heathcliff's desire to have his dead body blended with Catherine's, his going with blind joy to his death because he senses her presence calling him, and the vision which the shepherd boy sees and Nelly later senses, of the dead lovers reunited on the heath. Yet it is in paradoxically religious terms that, towards his death, Heathcliff speaks of the coming reconciliation: 'I'm too happy, and yet I'm not happy enough. My soul's bliss kills my body, but does not satisfy itself', and 'I tell you, I have nearly attained *my* heaven; and that of others is altogether unvalued and uncoveted by me!' (Chap. XXXIV, pp. 411 and 412).

It is reasonable to see this mutual yearning as a yearning not so much to possess each other (though that is how it appears in life) but rather to be made free, each through the other, of his own identity and of the universe. Perhaps not a 'transcendent reality', but at any rate a passion for self-transcendence.

The dying Heathcliff echoes the language of the living Catherine, and his attitude to her seems to be the same as hers to him. Yet the earlier and more violent expressions of his feeling, expressions both in language and in deed, are significantly different. And the fact raises what I take to be the central critical question, the question of the figure which Heathcliff cuts in the drama. It is perhaps significant that we see far less of Heathcliff while he has a relationship with a living, breathing Catherine than we do when he is ruthlessly bent on securing her ghost; and, consequently, we see, we have dramatically presented to us, less of his attitude to *her* than of his attitude to a world which, because of her death, has become for him 'a dreadful collection of memoranda that she did exist, and that I have lost her'. In fact, Heathcliff, in his relationship not only to Catherine but to their common world, is the book's centre; as Klingopulos says, 'The feelings of Catherine towards Heathcliff are different from his towards her; and her feelings are more than feelings towards him. They are feelings towards life and death'. Heathcliff, in fact, strikes us as imprisoned in his own consciousness, his own purposes, in a way that Catherine is not; and it may not be too fanciful to see her as, at the end of the novel, redeeming him from that imprisonment, opening out his emotions so that they are no longer simply fixated on her. She may be seen as taking spiritual initiatives which he cannot take; but he is still a much more substantial figure, a more substantial dramatic presence, in the drama of the book as a whole. It is, in my opinion, the very brooding constancy of his presence which presents the critical problem. It forces Brontë to try and maintain a dual balance: *First,* a balance between Heathcliff's positive feelings for Catherine and for her world, and his negative, destructive feelings for them (between all that is comprised by the psychic harmony and all that is suggested in the so-called purpose of revenge); and *Second,* a balance between Heathcliff as a recognizable human figure and Heathcliff as a symbol of earthy or cosmic forces (between a man with identifiable, definable motives, and a presence, a phenomenon, embodying certain forces). I am not sure she has kept this very delicate dual balance.

He is a more recognizably human figure than one at first thinks; but the great power with which Brontë invests him as a dramatic presence comes from the fact that we are aware of him more as a force than as a person. It is not merely that, in the central chapters, his day-to-day motives are hard to work out, and his attitude to Catherine's unfeigned joy at seeing him again remains one of hatred and destruction; it is also that, from the very beginning, he has been given a power which seems not wholly identifiable in human terms. That is a power so resonant with the forces of the earth that we can readily believe Catherine's feelings for him to be also feelings for those forces. The relationship, in short, (so the writing suggests) is not only a relationship between one person and another but also a relationship between each of them and the world of natural forces which each of them appears to represent to the other.

Admittedly, this is not merely a relationship between two persons, imaged by natural forces, but a relationship between each of them and the natural forces which each images to the other; and, admittedly, the triple relationship is in every way central to the web of relationships which the book creates, so that Brontë's achievement is not only to have established something important about possibilities in human nature but also to have suggested, by a play of natural images and analogies, something about human destiny. But this complexity would have been impossible if the person-to-person relationship, and the resemblance to natural forces on which it rests, had not been so powerful and profound.

In each of them this resemblance is so important that neither a process of 'civilizing' nor the assumption of adult tasks and responsibilities can destroy it. It is particularly strong in the case of Heathcliff.

And we almost suspect that Brontë is forcing us to recognize it. He has no known origins. When we first see him, he ('it') is carried like a shivering animal in Mr Earnshaw's greatcoat. He looks like an untamed gipsy even after he has acquired the superficial mannerisms of a gentleman. That part of his life in which he acquires those mannerisms is as obscure and mysterious as his parentage. The other characters often ask if he is human at all, and they ask it as no merely rhetorical question. His motives are hard to identify, and certainly we cannot account for his later actions by invoking the too-easy notion of 'revenge'. He has no Christian name, and he is referred to always by a name which is a compound of two natural things, heath and cliff. And when Cathy wants to say in what way she loves him, her use of natural analogies is such that we feel she is almost saying in what way she loves the universe of natural forces. One senses that he is both person and force, human and non-human. In Brontë's depiction of him, the methods of the novelist and those of the dramatic poet are oddly combined. The novelist usually analyses thoughts and motives or points to them by analysing behaviour; Heathcliff's thoughts are known to us by his actions and by his speeches; but both of these are so foreign to our expectations that we cannot build up a plausible notion of his motives. However delicately we go about the work of supplying an analysis, it is his quality as a force, a presence, a phenomenon which, by so impressing us, defeats it.

If we ask, then, about his view of his relationship with Catherine, it is hard to give an answer. But it is at least plain that his view is different from hers. We might have supposed from 'Catherine's declarations that *her* love is quite a-sexual; Heathcliff is in no doubt about the sexual nature of *his*. For her, their psychic harmony is such that separation is, in a sense, impossible; but for him, it is not only possible, it is the torment of torments. She can rest delighted in her love while married to another man; for him, a union between them is so patently dictated by their very natures that he must possess her in the fullest way. It is only in child-hood, then, that their love was idyllic; in its later stages, it is the torments which are insisted on rather than the satisfactions. Catherine is not only Heathcliff's heaven, she is his hell.

It seems to me that only if one postulates such large differences in the conceptions of their love are Heathcliff's brutalities intelligible. No doubt puzzles remain about his motives; but to say that his chief later motive is one of 'revenge' is surely to cheapen it. The motive, dimly apprehended even by himself, seemed to be to dominate a world in which Catherine has not only betrayed him but has left on every person and thing the imprint of her spirit.

We cannot, however, judge him in any external moralizing

fashion; for, even if we rightly discount the sufferings of his early boyhood, we remember that he is the object of Catherine's elevating passion, and see that the stature conferred upon him by the lyrical expressions of that passion is greatly heightened by his sufferings as an adult, caused as they are in part by his own temperament but in part also by her wilfulness. If his motives are obscure, the scope of his personality is, in the Shakespearean sense, tragic:

> 'I have neither a fear, nor a presentiment.... I am swallowed up in the anticipation of its fulfilment.' (Chap. XXXIII, p. 401) [*Please find the passage and read it through*]

And he sees his reunion with Catherine in terms of the natural scenes and energies of the Heights, just as she had earlier.

I am inclined to think that, if we look for the explanation of Heathcliff's motives as the actions they prompt are actually before us, we shall find only confusion. The actions are to be estimated in retrospect, in the perspective provided both by the speeches and by his behaviour in this final scene. Here again the affinity with Shakespeare is noticeable. Yet we *are* horrified by his brutalities as he commits them; we judge them to be evilly inappropriate to the nature of the harmony which both Catherine and he say they feel. We judge them, but we do not judge him; the Shakespearean dimensions of the drama as a whole will not allow us to. And those dimensions also lead us, despite Heathcliff's brutality and Catherine's wilfulness, despite our own comfortable expectations, despite the anathemas of Nelly and Isabella and the amazement of Lockwood, to endorse the Wuthering Heights view of the Lintons and their household. . . .

While Emily Brontë's passion has gone into the presentation of the lovers, her tough self-awareness has gone into Nelly Dean. It would be sentimental to regard Nelly as the book's moral centre; but it would be foolish to ignore or devalue the force which she has and which she represents. And we may remind ourselves that it is she, after all, who lays out Heathcliff's body for burial:

> Having succeeded in obtaining entrance with another key....
> Taken with another fit of cowardice, I cried out for Joseph.
> (Chap. XXXIV, p. 414) [*Please find the passage and read it through*]

She may complacently misunderstand the nature of their mutual passion, but she is able to testify, better than anyone else, that it was a passion of extraordinary intensity and great stature, which, nevertheless, remains in certain aspects puzzling to us as well as to her.

From *The Southern Review*, vol. I. No. 2, 1964, pp. 5–23.

WADE THOMPSON

Infanticide and Sadism in *Wuthering Heights*

This article will offer an interpretation of *Wuthering Heights* based upon the extraordinary sadism which underlies Emily Brontë's concept of emotional relationships and indicate the significance of her preoccupation with infanticide. Unless one appreciates the importance of infanticide and sadism in *Wuthering Heights,* one cannot appreciate the nature of the love between Catherine and Heathcliff, a love which I believe to have been frequently misunderstood, nor can one understand the motivation behind Heathcliff's killing of his own son. My chief contention is that *Wuthering Heights* is basically a perverse book—I use the word without its usual pejorative connotations—and that its power is owing precisely to its perversity.

I

In the first place, we may note that the children in *Wuthering Heights,* like the children in the Brontë household, are left to fend for themselves early in life without the love or protection of their mothers. Catherine Earnshaw is not quite eight when her mother dies; Cathy Linton's birth coincides with her mother's death; Hareton's mother dies in the year of his birth; and Heathcliff is an orphan by the time he is seven. Even the children who receive motherly care throughout their childhood do not receive it long after they reach puberty. Linton Heathcliff loses his mother when he is not quite thirteen—Linton, of course, is a child all his life—and Isabella Linton is orphaned when she is fourteen. The only exceptions—and these unimportant—are Hindley Earnshaw and Edgar Linton, who are sixteen and eighteen respectively when their mothers die (and even their mothers are apparently not very 'motherly').

Without the care of their mothers, the children find themselves in a fierce struggle for survival against actively hostile adults who seem obsessed with the desire to kill or maim them. From Lockwood's early dream of pulling the wrist of the ghostchild Catherine along a jagged window ledge, to Heathcliff's presiding with delight over the death of his overgrown child, the novel plays a multitude of insistent variations on the ghastly theme of infanticide. When Heathcliff is brought as a boy to the Earnshaw home, Mrs Earnshaw's first reaction is to

'fling it out of doors'. That night even the fairly kind-hearted
Nelly Dean puts 'it' on the landing in the hope that 'it might be gone
on the morrow'. Later, old Mr Linton apprehends 'it' prowling about
with Catherine near Thrushcross Grange and immediately proclaims,
'It is but a boy... would it not be a kindness to the country to hang
him at once?'... Isabella Linton puts this sentiment in her own
childish terms: 'Frightful thing! Put him in the cellar, papa.'

The infant Hareton Earnshaw lives in much greater danger.
Hindley's first instinct when drunk is to kill his son, whom Nelly
Dean constantly hides. At one time Heathcliff accidentally rescues
Hareton from a fall, but is so incensed by the mistake that 'had it been
dark... he would have tried to remedy the mistake by smashing
Hareton's skull on the steps'. Later Heathcliff is possessed by an
irrepressible desire to 'twist' the life of Hareton: 'We'll see if one
tree won't grow as crooked as another,' he says, and Nelly Dean thinks
that Hareton's natural 'soil' might have yielded 'luxuriant crops' without such deliberate stunting.

Hareton manages somehow to survive, but Linton Heathcliff is slowly
tortured to death by his father, whose desire to kill him is overwhelm-
ing: 'Had I been born where laws are less strict and tastes less dainty,
I should treat myself to a slow vivisection of those two [Linton and
Cathy] as an evening's amusement.'...

The infanticide theme is amplified symbolically throughout the
novel in the killing of helpless and delicate animals. Early in the
story Lockwood finds a heap of dead rabbits in the Heathcliff household. On one occasion, Isabella knocks over Hareton, 'who was hanging a litter of puppies from a chair-back'. Heathcliff shows Isabella
what kind of man he is by hanging her little pet springer. In her
death-bed delirium, Catherine recalls how she and Heathcliff saw a
lapwing's nest 'full of little skeletons. Heathcliff set a trap over it, and
the old ones dare not come'. Linton Heathcliff's favourite sport is to
torture to death cats whose claws and teeth have been pulled.

The killing of helpless animals forms the basis of numerous metaphors. Thus Edgar Linton could no more leave Catherine than a cat
could 'leave a mouse half killed, or a bird half eaten'. Isabella in
Heathcliff's hands is like 'a little canary in the park on a winter's
day'. Or again, Hindley Earnshaw is like a 'stray sheep' which 'God
had forsaken', and Heathcliff is 'an evil beast' which 'prowled between it and the fold'.

Directly and indirectly, then, Emily Brontë envisions a world in
which the young and the weak live in constant peril....

As Leicester Bradner has pointed out, Emily Brontë seems to have
been obsessed with the vision of a young, lovely, happy child growing
up to a life of misery and/or crime. Death for the child would clearly

be better than life.[1] Poem after poem expresses the sense of an experience having the force of absolute possession, known in childhood, and recoverable only in death—as though infanticide has a kind of religious justification. Thus death and childhood are firmly linked in Emily Brontë's chain of associations.

Another link in the chain is the prevalence of pain as an elementary condition of life. In *Wuthering Heights,* the wild eruptions of cruelty and violence are so vivid that one tends not to notice how frequently pain is inflicted just as a matter of course. Pinching, slapping, and hair pulling occur constantly. Catherine wakes Nelly Dean up, not by shaking her gently, but by pulling her hair. Nelly Dean hears a 'manual check' given to Cathy's saucy mouth. When Catherine first dined at the Linton's, she was 'as merry as she could be, dividing her food between the little dog and Skulker, whose nose she pinched as he ate; and kindling a spark of spirit in the vacant blue eyes of the Lintons'. Later she is so joyous that 'should the meanest thing alive slap me on the cheek, I'd not only turn the other, but, I'd ask pardon for provoking it'.

Pain, inflicted by cutting or stabbing, forms the crux of numerous metaphors. Nelly Dean speaks of a 'frosty air that cut about her shoulders as keen as a knife'. On one occasion, Isabella shrieked 'as if witches were running red-hot needles into her'. When Hareton timidly put out a hand to stroke one of Cathy's curls, 'he might have struck a knife into her neck, she started round in such a taking'. Linton 'averred that the stab of a knife could not inflict a worse pang than he suffered at seeing his lady vexed'.

In like manner, pain is frequently suggested by threats of choking, throttling, suffocating, or strangling. Thus Linton Heathcliff always on the verge of 'choking', does not want Cathy to kiss him because he is afraid of losing his breath. Heathcliff threatens to 'strangle' Cathy if she won't be quiet. Even adjectives and verbs suggest choking. The falling snow is 'suffocating'. Hareton 'smothered the storm in a brutal curse'. Visitors are 'smothered in cloaks and furs'.

In summary, then, the world of *Wuthering Heights* is a world of sadism, violence, and wanton cruelty, wherein the children—without the protection of their mothers—have to fight for very life against adults who show almost no tenderness, love, or mercy. Normal emotions are almost completely inverted: hate replaces love, cruelty replaces kindness, and survival depends on one's ability to be tough, brutal, and rebellious.

[1] Leicester Bradner 'The Growth of *Wuthering Heights*,' *P.M.L.A.*, Vol. XLVIII, 1933, pp.129-46.

II

When one considers the almost unbearable danger of pain and death to which children are subject in *Wuthering Heights*, one is struck by the terrible irony of the fact that, after her death, Catherine wishes to return—and indeed does return—not as an adult, but as a child. . . . As a child Catherine is endowed with a kind of masculine power that only the most hardened adults usually possess; she has most unchild-like resources for self-control, endurance, and sustained rebellion; and she can easily cope with pain. Her choice of toy is a whip. . . .

At the same time Heathcliff proves to be so self-possessed that he too is beyond intimidation by pain or suffering. When Hindley fells him with an iron weight over the argument about colts, Nelly Dean is surprised 'to witness how coolly the child gathered himself up, and went on with his intention; exchanging saddles and all, and then sitting down on a bundle of hay to overcome the qualm which the violent blow occasioned, before he entered the house'.

Together these almost monstrous 'children' establish a mystic bond, forged in pain, and expressed in rebellion. They feel an absolute identification with each other. Heathcliff cannot imagine himself and Catherine behaving like Edgar Linton and Isabella: 'When would you catch me wishing to have what Catherine wanted? to find us by ourselves, seeing entertainment in yelling, and sobbing, and rolling on the ground, divided by the whole room?' And Catherine is just as dedicated. 'I am Heathcliff', she insists—and so long as she can fully identify with him, she is strong.

The intensity of their bond is frequently conveyed in suggestions of incest and child sexuality. Heathcliff may easily be Catherine's half-brother—at least we are invited to entertain that suspicion—and Catherine almost always uses the imagery of incest to express her love for Heathcliff: 'the same daemonic substance'. She and Heathcliff sleep together until she is over twelve years old, and she cries for the first time when Hindley separates them as bed partners.

The disintegration of Catherine's personality begins with the Thrushcross Grange episode. She fails to see that her entrance into puberty requires a radical change in her relation with Heathcliff, and cannot understand his behaviour after her return to Wuthering Heights. Her attitude towards him remains as it was before puberty, but he recoils 'with angry suspicion from her girlish caresses'. In his presence she exhibits the same masculine endurance of pain and contempt for weakness that had characterized her childhood. When Heathcliff dashes hot apple sauce in Edgar Linton's face, she blames Edgar for provoking him, adding, 'he'll be flogged; I hate him to be flogged! I can't eat my dinner', and she scorns Edgar's sobbing with the con-temptuous remark, 'well, don't cry . . . you're not killed'. She herself cries, in sympathy for Heathcliff, but only after a valiant effort to hold back the tears.

Even after her marriage, she is tough and masculine in the presence of Heathcliff. She contemns her husband for crying, scorns his 'whining for trifles' and 'idle petulance'. She takes Heathcliff's side in his climactic fight with Edgar, and her pitilessness is truly awesome. 'If you have not courage to attack him', she says to her husband, 'make an apology, or allow yourself to be beaten'.

The source of her strength, however, is Heathcliff. Without him, she gradually finds herself unable to endure pain or to keep her self-possession, and her temper becomes uncontrollable. During Edgar Linton's last visit to Wuthering Heights, she loses her poise in a dispute with Heathcliff, after which she pinches and slaps Nelly Dean, lies about it, shakes little Hareton 'till the poor child waxed livid', boxes Edgar on the ear, insists 'I did nothing deliberately', and begins weep-ing 'in serious earnest'. As she grows older, pain becomes intolerable; she cries on the slightest provocation and resorts easily to fits of petu-lance and self-pity. 'Our fiery Catherine was no better than a wailing child', remarks Nelly Dean of the grown woman who could 'beat Hareton, or any child, at a good passionate fit of crying'.

Her marriage to Linton serves only to weaken her, and the open break between Heathcliff and Linton finally destroys her completely. She resorts to 'senseless, wicked rages'. 'There she lay dashing her head against the arm of the sofa, and grinding her teeth, so that you might fancy she would crash them to splinters.' The girl who could once hold off a whole household of angry adults now loses all self-possession. She imagines that everyone is against her: 'I thought, though everybody hated and despised each other, they could not avoid loving me. And they have all turned to enemies in a few hours: *they* have, I'm positive; the people *here*.' Her fantasies are almost as terrify-ing as her dreams, and her dreams 'appal' her. By this time she has completely lost her grip on reality. She sees a face in the black press which isn't there. 'Oh! Nelly, the room is haunted! I'm afraid of being alone!'

In the brief life of Catherine, then, there is a complete reversal of roles. As a child she is an adult; even her sauciness is grounded in inner strength. As an adult she becomes a child, and the pain of living proves intolerable. 'I wish I were a girl again', she cries pathetically, 'half savage and hardy, and free; and laughing at injuries, not madden-ing under them'. She remembers that she was once strong and knows she is strong no longer. Logically enough, therefore, in her ghostly state, she assumes the role, not of a lovely lady in the lonely moors

calling for her lover (which would surely be the 'romantic' expecta-
tion), but of a little girl come back 'home'.

III

While Catherine's return in the role of a child fulfils her yearning
to regain her childhood strength, it also betrays the fact that only as a
child was she ever able to love Heathcliff. After puberty, she is never
able to transform her childish passion for identity ('I am Heathcliff',
she says—but one does not mate with one's self, with one's kind)
into a passion for the union of opposites. Her marriage to Linton, a
weak, respectable, undemanding person, is essentially an escape from
the demands of adult sexuality, and she sees no betrayal of Heathcliff
in the escape. To her, Heathcliff is, and always will be, her wild
'childhood' lover; Linton is her respectable 'adult' lover, and the two
are perfectly compatible. She is never jealous of Heathcliff and cannot
understand his jealousy of her; she simply thinks of her 'love' for him
as entirely different from her 'love' for Linton.

Indeed she is correct. The 'love' she can offer Heathcliff is precisely
the love she offered him as a child—tough, masculine 'identity', born
in pain, expressed in pain—but nothing like normal adult love: no
eroticism, no sex, no pleasure, no satisfaction. *Her* 'love' is expressed
through pain, hate, and relentless recrimination. Hair-pulling and
pinching are her modes of physical expression. Surely no more
sexless and abnormal scene can be imagined than the final love scene
between herself and Heathcliff: 'I shouldn't care what you suffered.
I care nothing for your sufferings. Why shouldn't *you* suffer?' she
says to him. And he can only respond in kind: 'Is it not sufficient
for your infernal selfishness, that while you are at peace I shall writhe
in the torments of hell?' They can meet only in pain and distress:
'should a word of mine distress you hereafter, think I feel the same
distress underground'.

Because Catherine had been unable to meet the demands of adult
sexuality, Heathcliff takes revenge by imposing adult sexuality on
children, her child and his. The 'love' between Linton and Cathy is the
ghastly obverse of the love between their parents. Whereas the parents
were passionately devoted to each other but could find no fulfilling
means of expression, the young ones have the means of expression
forced upon them even though they find each other totally repulsive.
Linton cannot endure women. At one point having been tortured
enough with Cathy's presence, he is granted permission—to his unspeakable relief—to sleep with Hareton. Eventually, however, Linton
is killed. The revenge is complete.

IV

With the killing of Linton, the terrible implications of the infanticide theme become clear: since childhood is the source of perversity, children are quite logically feared, hated, and finally killed. It was the 'child' in Catherine that destroyed the love between her and Heathcliff; it is the 'child' in Linton that Heathcliff hates: he imposes adult 'love' on his son and Cathy with the full knowledge that such love is absolutely unendurable. An eye for an eye, a tooth for a tooth.

The great love story of *Wuthering Heights* then, begins in perversity and ends in perversity. The 'love' between Catherine and Heathcliff grows under the terrible threat of infanticide, never undergoes a metamorphosis into maturity, and so culminates in revenge on the next generation. The only escape is death; and both Catherine and Heathcliff deeply yearn to die. 'The thing that irks me most is this shattered prison, after all', says Catherine. 'I'm tired of being enclosed here. I'm wearying to escape into that glorious world, and to be always there . . . really with it, and in it.' And Heathcliff is just as eager for death. As soon as he has killed his son, he deliberately wills his own death. These people take the measure of life and choose to die, simply because life offers no fulfilment. In the end, the shepherd boy sees 'Heathcliff and a woman' (no longer a child) now roaming freely and happily about the moors. But such a consummation could never come in life. Life is pain, hate, and perversity. It is a tribute to Emily Brontë's uncanny poetic powers that she has deceived generations of readers into believing that they were reading a beautiful, romantic, and indeed glorious love story.

From *P.M.L.A.*, vol. LXXVII, No. 1, 1963, pp. 69–74.
Several footnotes have been omitted.

J. HILLIS MILLER

Themes of Isolation and Exile

. . . The violence of Emily Brontë's characters is a reaction to the loss of an earlier state of happiness. Heathcliff's situation at the beginning of *Wuthering Heights* is the same as the situation of many characters in Emily Brontë's poems, and the refrain of both poems and novel is 'Never again' (P. 64).[1]

[1] This and subsequent numbers refer to the pages in C. W. Hatfield's *Poems of Emily Brontë*, N.Y., 1941.

This state of loss is dramatized in many of the poems as the longing in harshest wintertime for the vanished warmth of mid-summer weather, or as the memory of an earlier time of happy love, ecstatic visions, or unity with nature. The sense of bereavement is often expressed as a condition of exile, imprisonment, or separation, or in terms of the grief of the living for the dead. The Gondal saga was apparently a species of prose epic, of which we possess only the lyric poems which were interspersed here and there in the narrative. These usually pick out some moment of special poignancy or significance, and dramatize it in the speech of the person who experiences it. Most often the moment chosen is not the time of joy, but the moment of sorrow, exile, or defeat. It seems as if all the elaborate machinery of the Gondal saga had been contrived as a means of expressing repeatedly, in different forms, one universal experience of absolute destitution:

> I know that tonight the wind is sighing,
> The soft August wind, over forest and moor;
> While I in a grave-like chill am lying
> On the damp black flags of my dungeon-floor. (P. 234, 235)

> Light up thy halls! 'Tis closing day;
> I'm drear and lone and far away—
> Cold blows on my breast the northwind's bitter sigh,
> And oh, my couch is bleak beneath the rainy sky! (P. 85)

Such people are suffering the anguish of irremediable loss. Their eyes are fixed backward in retrospective fascination on some past moment of sovereign joy. Only in that moment were they really alive, really themselves. Their present lives are determined by the loss of some past joy, and by the suffering caused by that loss. Such people live separated from themselves, and yearn with impotent violence to regain their lost happiness.

The fundamental dramatic situation of the poems reappears again in *Wuthering Heights*. Like a Gondal character, Isabella longs to be back at Thrushcross Grange after her elopement with Heathcliff, just as Heathcliff is tormented after Catherine's death, and just as Catherine suffers after her marriage to Edgar Linton. 'But', she says, 'supposing at twelve years old, I had been wrenched from the Heights, and every early association, and my all in all, as Heathcliff was at that time, and had been converted, at a stroke into Mrs Linton, the lady of Thrushcross Grange, and the wife of a stranger; an exile, and outcast, thenceforth, from what had been my world—You may fancy a glimpse of the abyss where I grovelled!'. And Heathcliff cries out to the ghost of Cathy: 'Be with me always—take any form—drive me mad! only *do* not leave me in this abyss, where I cannot find you! Oh, God!

it is unutterable! I *cannot* live without my life! I *cannot* live without my soul!'

For Emily Brontë no human being is self-sufficient, and all suffering derives ultimately from isolation. A person is most himself when he participates most completely in the life of something outside himself. This self outside the self is the substance of a man's being, in both the literal and etymological senses of the word. It is the intimate stuff of the self, and it is also that which 'stands beneath' the self as its foundation and support. A man's real being is outside himself. Emily Brontë's writings are an exploration of the consequences of this strange situation. . . .

Though heaven is man's final goal, Emily Brontë's poems and her novel are concerned initially with life on this earth, and the chief example here of fusion with something outside the self is the profound communion of children or lovers. The crucial sentence of *Wuthering Heights* is Catherine's bold expression of the paradox of substance: 'I *am* Heathcliff.' Heathcliff, Cathy says, is her being. Only so long as he exists will she continue to exist. Cathy defines her relation to Heathcliff not only in her striking formula, but also, in the surrounding sentences, in closely reasoned language, the most logical and explicit in the novel. Her explanation describes her relation to Heathcliff in the same terms Emily Brontë uses to define so lucidly the relation of the soul to God in 'No coward soul is mine'. Just as God, in the poem, is both within the soul and outside it, so, Cathy says, Heathcliff is at once within her and beyond her. He is the part of her that exists outside herself, and that part is her true self, her essence, more herself than she is. A created being entirely self-contained would have no use or meaning. Without a self beyond the self, 'an existence of yours beyond you', the self would be senseless and fragmentary. Heathcliff is to Cathy as necessary as the very ground she stands on, or, rather, as necessary as the eternal rocks beneath which support that ground. Heathcliff is both that which stands beneath her, and that which she intimately is: '. . . he's more myself than I am,' cries Cathy. 'Whatever our souls are made of, his and mine are the same . . . Who is to separate us, pray? . . . My love for Linton is like the foliage in the woods. Time will change it, I'm well aware, as winter changes the trees—my love for Heathcliff resembles the eternal rocks beneath—a source of little visible delight, but necessary. Nelly, I *am* Heathcliff—he's always, always in my mind—not as a pleasure, any more than I am always a pleasure to myself—but, as my own being. . . .'

Cathy affirms something more of her love for Heathcliff, something which has great importance for her life and his. In *No coward soul is mine* the essence of the soul is the God of whom one may say either that He is contained within the soul or that the soul is contained within

Him, and in the same way the essence of every created thing is contained in God:

> Though Earth and moon were gone
> And suns and universes ceased to be
> And thou wert left alone
> Every Existence would exist in thee . . . (P. 243)

In the novel Cathy asserts exactly this of Heathcliff. Her relation to Heathcliff gives her possession not merely of Heathcliff, but of the entire universe through him, in an intimacy of possession which obliterates the boundaries of the self and makes it an integral part of the whole creation. 'If all else perished', says Cathy, 'and *he* remained, I should still continue to be; and if all else remained, and he were annihilated, the Universe would turn to a mighty stranger. I should not seem a part of it'. . . .

Cathy and Heathcliff are as inseparably joined as trunk and root of the living tree. Their relation to one another excludes or absorbs their relation to everything else. Each is related to the rest of the universe only through the other. Through Heathcliff, Cathy possesses all of nature. Through Cathy, Heathcliff possesses it. . . .

To remain happy Cathy need only maintain her identification with Heathcliff. That identification seems invulnerable, for, as Cathy affirms, it will survive every vicissitude of her relations to others. Her love guarantees its own permanence. If the lovers endure, their love will endure untouched. If either is annihilated, then the other will also disappear. The existence of each is altogether determined by the other.

The love of Heathcliff and Cathy is not quite so simple as this. Between happy possession and annihilation stands a third dreadful possibility: the violent separation of the trunk from its root. If this happens the trunk may be forced to persist in a universe from which it has been dissevered. The intimate communion of all things with one another will perish with this disconnection. Then the universe will 'turn to a mighty stranger', and the unwilling survivor will not seem a part of it.

Lockwood finds just such a situation when he first comes to Wuthering Heights. It is Heathcliff who has survived Cathy rather than the other way around. His anguish at being forced to live with his soul in the grave has turned Wuthering Heights into a kennel of hatred and aggression. . . .

Heathcliff's Revenge

Heathcliff's situation after Cathy's death is different from hers while she lived, and his reaction to that situation is not the despairing acceptance of separateness, but the attempt to regain his lost fullness

of being. The universal human desire is for union with something outside oneself. People differ from one another only in the intensity of
their desire, and in the diversity of the ways they seek to assuage it.

After Cathy's death Heathcliff's whole life is concentrated on the
suffering caused by his loss, and on the violence of his desire to get
her back, for she is his soul, and without her he grovels in an abyss
of nothingness. Why does Heathcliff spend so much of his time in an
elaborate attempt to destroy Thrushcross Grange and Wuthering
Heights, with all their inhabitants? Why does he take delight in
torturing Hindley, Isabella, Hareton, the second Cathy, his son
Linton? Why does he, both before Cathy's death and after, enter on
a violent career of sadistic destruction? Is it because he is, as Cathy
says, a 'fierce, pitiless, wolfish man', or does his sadism have some
further meaning?

During the violent scene of mutual recrimination between Heathcliff and Cathy which ends in the fight between Heathcliff and Edgar,
Heathcliff tells Cathy that she has treated him 'infernally' by betraying
him and marrying Edgar. He will not, he says, 'suffer unrevenged'. But,
says Heathcliff, 'I seek no revenge on you . . . The tyrant grinds down
his slaves and they don't turn against him, they crush those beneath
them—You are welcome to torture me to death for your amusement,
only, allow me to amuse myself a little in the same style. . . .' Heathcliff's cruelty toward others is a mode of relation to Cathy. Though
his appearance at Wuthering Heights in itself disrupts the Earnshaw
family, Heathcliff's relation to Cathy forms the basis of his defiance
of everyone else, and his destructive hatred attains its full development
only after he is separated from her. His sadistic treatment of others is
the only kind of revenge against Cathy he can take, for the person who
most controls events in *Wuthering Heights* is not Heathcliff. It is
Cathy herself.

Heathcliff's sadism is more than an attempt to take revenge indirectly
on Cathy. It is also a strange and paradoxical attempt to regain his
lost intimacy with her. If Cathy can say, 'I *am* Heathcliff', Heathcliff
could equally well say, 'I *am* Cathy', for she is, as he says, his 'soul'.
Possession of Heathcliff gives Cathy possession of the entire universe.
If she were to lose Heathcliff, 'the universe would turn to a mighty
stranger', just as Heathcliff becomes an alien and outcast from all
the world after he loses Cathy. If his childhood relation to Cathy
gave him possession of the whole world through her, perhaps now
that Cathy is lost he can get her back by appropriating the world. The
sadistic infliction of pain on other people, like the destruction of
inanimate objects, is a way of breaking down the barriers between
oneself and the world. Now that he has lost Cathy, the only thing
remaining to Heathcliff which is like the lost fusion with her is the

destructive assimilation of other people or things. So he turns sadist, just as, in the Gondal poems, Julius Brenzaida turns on the world in war when he has been betrayed by Augusta. Heathcliff's violence against everyone but Cathy plays the same role in *Wuthering Heights* as does the theme of war in the poems. In both cases there is an implicit recognition that war or sadism is like love because love too is destructive, since it must break down the separateness of the loved one. Augusta too is a sadist. She moves quickly from inspiring her lovers to abandon honour for her sake to betraying them and causing them to suffer. Like love, sadism is a moment of communion, a moment when the barriers between person and person are broken down. The climax of sadistic joy is loss of the sense of separateness. It is as though the person who is forced to suffer had lost his limits and had melted into the whole universe. At the same moment the self of the sadist dissolves too, and self and universe become one. Heathcliff's relation to Cathy has been fusion with the whole world through her. He feels that he can reverse the process and regain her by assimilating the world, for his sole aim is to 'dissolve with' Cathy and be happy at last. Now he proposes to do this by getting control of Wuthering Heights and Thrushcross Grange in order to destroy them both. 'I wish', says Heathcliff of his property, 'I could annihilate it from the face of the earth'. So he gives himself whole-heartedly to acts of sadistic destruction. No other figure in English literature takes so much pleasure in causing pain to others: 'I have no pity! I have no pity!' he cries. 'The more the worms writhe, the more I yearn to crush out their entrails! It is a moral teething, and I grind with greater energy, in proportion to the increase of pain.' In another place he tells Nelly his feelings about his son and the second Cathy: 'It's odd what a savage feeling I have to anything that seems afraid of me! Had I been born where laws are less strict, and tastes less dainty, I should treat myself to a slow vivisection of those two, as an evening's amusement.'

Heathcliff's effort to regain Cathy through sadistic destruction fails, just as does Augusta's attempt to achieve through sadistic love a fusion with something outside herself, and just as does Cathy's decision to will her own death. Heathcliff's sadism fails because, as things or people are annihilated under the blows of the sadist, he is left with nothing. He reaches only an exacerbated sense of the absence of the longed-for intimacy rather than the intimacy itself. Augusta goes from lover to lover, destroying them one by one because she cannot reach what she wants through them. And Heathcliff finds that his career of sadistic revenge is a way of suffering the loss of Cathy more painfully rather than a way of reaching her again. 'It is a poor conclusion, is it not', he asks. 'An absurd termination to my violent exertions?

I get levers, and mattocks to demolish the two houses, and train myself to be capable of working like Hercules, and when everything is ready, and in my power, I find the will to lift a slate off either roof has vanished! . . . I have lost the faculty of enjoying their destruction. . . .'

The reason Heathcliff gives for having lost the will to demolish the two houses is a confirmation of the fact that his relation to everything in the world is a relation to Cathy, and an admission of the defeat of his attempt to regain her by destroying the Grange and the Heights. He says that everything in the universe is a reminder that Cathy has existed and that he does not possess her. Through his destruction of others he has reached, in the wreckage left after his violence, the full realization of her absence: '. . . what is not connected with her to me?' he asks, 'and what does not recall her? I cannot look down to this floor, but her features are shaped in the flags! In every cloud, in every tree—filling the air at night, and caught by glimpses in every object, by day I am surrounded with her image! The most ordinary faces of men, and women—my own features mock me with a resemblance. The entire world is a dreadful collection of memoranda that she did exist, and that I have lost her!' The universe is identified not with Cathy, but with the absence of Cathy, and to possess the world through its destructive appropriation is not to possess Cathy, but to confront once more the vacant place where she is not. This is the hell in which Heathcliff lives after her death: 'I could *almost* see her, and yet I *could not!* I ought to have sweat blood then, from the anguish of my yearning, from the fervour of my supplications to have but one glimpse! I had not one. She showed herself, as she often was in life, a devil to me! And, since then, sometimes more, and sometimes less, I've been the sport of that intolerable torture!' Heathcliff's sadistic tormenting of others only leads him to be the more tormented, tormented by a Cathy whose strongest weapon is her invisibility. . . .

From the chapter on Emily Brontë in *The Disappearance of God: Five Nineteenth Century Writers,* The Belknap Press of Harvard University Press, Cambridge, Mass., O. U. P., London, 1963, pp. 155–211. Subtitles by the editor. [This is a particularly original and stimulating essay.]

MARY VISICK

Emily Brontë's Poetry

... [*Wuthering Heights*] represents a reworking of the material of Emily Brontë's poems, but these are not the mere débris of the novel: she was, indeed, a remarkable poet. Some would claim that she was a great one. She cut through the quickset hedge of romantic quasi-Miltonic diction—it is hard to realize that she was a contemporary of Tennyson—to a cold, clear simplicity which has affinities with the diction of Wordsworth, whom she almost certainly read, and that of Blake, whom it seems unlikely that she knew.

There is little 'development' to be traced in her verse, though it extends over a period of more than ten years. There is rather a progressive clarification of certain themes—for example, the setting of human experience in a great landscape, a vision of a lonely, haunted child, death and lamentation. It is well known that Emily Brontë lived a great part of her adult life with a dream-world which she constructed with her sister Anne and called Gondal. They peopled it with wild and elemental characters whose stories they recorded in a series of prose 'books' which have not survived (they may have been destroyed by Charlotte or by her husband, by Emily herself or by Anne after Emily's death). The complications of the Gondal references occasionally make Emily Brontë's poetry appear freakish and even childish; but, tempting though it is to see in her work a progressive emancipation from Gondal, it remains true that the fantasy produced some beautifully-wrought poetry, much of which, recording as it does lyric moments in the Gondal saga, can be valued for its own sake. Such are the exquisite double lyric which Charlotte called *The Two Children,* the famous lament *Cold in the Earth,* and *The Prisoner.* Emily Brontë is not justly estimated if she is known only as the author of half a dozen familiar pieces; her collected poems reveal her as a fine craftsman, and each poem is 'made' with deliberation. Many of the earliest-dated pieces are mere fragments which she did not transcribe into the two books which she kept for fair copies but which, on the other hand, she did not destroy. They are sketches for fully finished poems—for example:

> Woods, you need not frown on me;
> Spectral trees, that so dolefully

> Shake your heads in the dreary sky,
> You need not mock so bitterly.[1]

or, a year later, when she was in her twentieth year, we find an exquisite note:

> Only some spires of bright green grass
> Transparently in sunlight quivering.[2]

A complete poem written when she was nineteen—an unglossed, unexplained dramatic lyric—will serve to illustrate how far from adolescent exuberance are Emily Brontë's earliest lines; the management of the disyllabic rhymes is serenely competent, and the poem hardly reads like 'prentice work:

> The night is darkening round me,
> The wild winds coldly blow;
> But a tyrant spell has bound me
> And I cannot, cannot go.
>
> The giant trees are bending
> Their bare boughs weighed with snow,
> And the storm is fast descending
> And yet I cannot go.
>
> Clouds beyond clouds above me,
> Wastes beyond wastes below;
> But nothing drear can move me;
> I will not, cannot go.[3]

Already we feel the mind in pursuit of the clarifying word. Twelve months after she wrote this poem, Emily Brontë was at Law Hill, working as a school-teacher under conditions which her indignant older sister described as 'slavery'. Here at last her fortitude broke down; the agonies of homesickness might have been poured out in desperate verse. Instead, the artist who creates separates herself from the woman who suffers; and the poem in which she puts down her thoughts of home has the serenity of perfect re-creation:

> . . . The house is old, the trees are bare
> And moonless bends the misty dome
> But what on earth is half so dear,
> So longed for as the hearth of home?
>
> The mute bird sitting on the stone,
> The dank moss dripping from the wall,
> The garden-walk with weeds o'ergrown,
> I love them—how I love them all! . . .

---

[1] Hatfield, No. 6   [2] Hatfield, No. 20.   [3] Hatfield, No. 36

> A little and a lone green lane
> That opened on a common wide;
> A distant, dreamy, dim blue chain
> Of mountains circling every side;
>
> A heaven so clear, an earth so calm,
> So sweet, so soft, so hushed an air
> And, deepening still the dream-like charm,
> Wild moor-sheep feeding everywhere ... [1]

It is not a far cry from this to the pieces which are deservedly familiar; read in their context, as the latest and most finished expressions of her insights, they gain in importance. Among the later poems, too, are several which deserve to be more widely known: for example, the one she afterwards called *Stars*, or the cryptic, Blake-like '*Enough of thought, philosopher*'. ...

The Gondal Poems and *Wuthering Heights*

Two [of the later Gondal poems] concern Julius, of which one is Rosina's lament *Cold in the earth, and the deep snow piled above thee* ... which has struck many readers as prefiguring the eighteen years of Heathcliff's mourning for Catherine. However another poem which also occurs late in the manuscript is even closer in verbal expression to Heathcliff; and here, as in *No coward soul* ... the reference is not to ordinary human love but to some other order of experience. It is a long Gondal narrative of which some self-contained stanzas were published in the 1846 volume as *The Prisoner, a fragment*:

> Then dawns the Invisible, the Unseen its truth reveals;
> My outward sense is gone, my inward essence feels—
> Its wings are almost free, its home, its harbour found;
> Measuring the gulf it stoops and dares the final bound!
>
> Oh, dreadful is the check—intense the agony
> When the ear begings to hear, and the eye begins to see;
> When the pulse begins to throb, the brain to think again, ·
> The soul to feel the flesh, and the flesh to feel the chain. [2]

In *Wuthering Heights* Heathcliff's dead love, or rather the sense of her presence, is at the core of the invisible world he cannot reach:

> 'I have neither a fear, nor a presentiment, nor a hope of death. Why should I? With my hard constitution and temperate mode of living, and unperilous occupation, I ought to, and probably *shall* remain above ground, till there is scarcely a black hair on my

[1] Hatfield, No. 92.
[2] The whole poem is Hatfield, No. 190.

head—And yet I cannot continue in this condition! I have to
remind myself to breathe—almost to remind my heart to beat!
And it is like bending back a stiff spring: it is by compulsion
that I do the slightest act not prompted by one thought, and by
compulsion that I notice anything alive or dead, which is not
associated with one universal idea. I have a single wish, and my
whole being and faculties are yearning to attain it. They have
yearned towards it so long, and so unwaveringly, that I'm convinced it *will* be reached—and soon—because it has devoured my
existence: I am swallowed up in the anticipation of its fulfilment . . . O, God! It is a long fight, I wish it were over.'[1]

Here is [an] . . . indication that the love between Catherine and Heathcliff is Emily Brontë's way of giving expression to some all-devouring
spiritual experience. . . .

That her story had its rise in some personal experience seems most
likely. When speaking of such a writer, whose outer life looks both
meagre and satisfactory (kneading the Parsonage bread with her
German grammar stuck up over the trough, picking fruit, feeding
the animals) and whose inner life is revealed only in hints and glimpses, we are not likely to put a crude interpretation on the word
'experience'. What is recorded in the central stanzas of *The Prisoner*
is clearly as real as anything that could happen to the outward form
of 't' Parson's Emily'. The god whom she addresses in her poems
is a creedless, immortal energy. Presumably the parson's daughter paid
her formal respects to Christianity, but the mystical experiences of
this sense of infinity and immortality are not, in her poetry, couched
in Christian terms or given Christian explanations. She sought to find
expression for them not through orthodox religion but through the
fantasy of Gondal. We have seen how closely Catherine's expression
of her identity with Heathcliff echoes *No coward soul* . . . and that
Heathcliff's longing for Catherine is like the Prisoner's agony as she is
dragged back to the life of the senses. Somewhere in this realm of her
consciousness there was formed some kind of experience of the strife
between night and day, between the cool and gentle and the hot and
vital.

There are at least three attempts to express this strife in words.
Two try to express it in terms of human personalities clashing; she is
feeling her way towards it in the modifications of the Lord Alfred
story in Gondal and she sets it out at length in *Wuthering Heights*.
The third attempt is in a poem written in 1845 and called, in the 1846
volume, *Stars*. Its relation to Gondal suggests that is more than a

---

[1] *Wuthering Heights*, Chapter XXXIII.

'nature-lyric', that it is in fact a developed symbol for destructive vitality. The visionary may seek out the night, but inevitably morning comes. So Catherine may seek out the soul of Edgar which she compares to moonlight and frost, but she cannot escape the lightning and fire of Heathcliff. Let us not commit the crudity of looking in Emily Brontë's biography for some kind of emotional upheaval: the poem is self-consistent and self-explanatory, and incidentally it utters a warning to any critic who would draw an absolute dividing line between the Gondal and the non-Gondal verse. The poet herself copied it into the non-Gondal volume, but perhaps she could not have written it were it not for the preliminary sketches of the theme (*I gazed upon the cloudless moon* . . . and so on) which belong to Gondal. Only through the Gondal people, perhaps, could Emily Brontë realize her vision, but *Stars* is emancipated from Gondal:

> Ah! why, because the dazzling sun
> Restored my earth to joy
> Have you departed, every one,
> And left a desert sky?
>
> All through the night, your glorious eyes
> Were gazing down in mine,
> And with a full heart's thankful sighs
> I blessed that watch divine!
>
> I was at peace, and drank your beams
> As they were life to me
> And revelled in my changeful dreams
> Like petrel on the sea.
>
> Thought followed thought—star followed star
> Through boundless regions on,
> While one sweet influence, near and far,
> Thrilled through and made us one.
>
> Why did the morning rise to break
> So great, so pure a spell,
> And scorch with fire the tranquil cheek
> Where your cool radiance fell?
>
> Blood-red he rose, and arrow-straight
> His fierce beams struck my brow:
> The soul of Nature sprang elate,
> But mine sank sad and low!
>
> My lids closed down—yet through their veil
> I saw him blazing still;
> And bathe in gold the misty dale,
> And flash upon the hill.

I turned me to the pillow then
To call back Night, and see
Your worlds of solemn light, again
Throb with my heart and me!

It would not do—the pillow glowed
And glowed both roof and floor,
And birds sang loudly in the wood,
And fresh winds shook the door.

The curtains waved, the wakened flies
Were murmuring round my room,
Imprisoned there, till I should rise
And give them leave to roam.

O Stars and Dreams and Gentle Night;
O Night and Stars return!
And hide me from the hostile light
That does not warm, but burn—

That drains the blood of suffering men;
Drinks tears, instead of dew:
Let me sleep through his blinding reign,
And only wake with you![1]

Miss Ratchford [in *Gondal's Queen*. See Bibliography] takes this as a straight Gondal monologue; but its author did not call it a Gondal poem. It is indeed, like the central stanzas of *The Prisoner*, a poem which suggests that Gondal had served its purpose. The poet no longer needs to wear the mask of A.G.A. [the heroine of the Gondal saga], and nowhere does that passionate but uncomplicated young woman speak with the voice of this poem. It is the quintessence of the Gondal situation, but, paradoxically, once she had grasped the means of expressing it Emily Brontë ceased to need the Gondal people. For the most part they disappeared, but the moments in which they lived most intensely were regrouped, and out of the regrouping rose *Wuthering Heights*, in which the central Gondal people themeselves were reborn as Catherine, Heathcliff and Edgar, Cathy, Hareton and Isabella. . . .

From *The Genesis of 'Wuthering Heights'*, Hong Kong University Press, Hong Kong, 1958, 2nd ed., 1965, pp. 1–5, 15–16, 35–8.

[1] Hatfield, No. 184.

SELECT BIBLIOGRAPHY

THE WORKS OF CHARLOTTE AND EMILY BRONTË

The most comprehensive edition is the *Shakespeare Head Brontë*, (ed.). T. J. Wise and J. A. Symington, 19 vols., Oxford, 1931–8. Other editions are the *Haworth*, 1899–1903; the *Temple*, 1893, new ed. 1905, repr. 1938; the *Thornton*, 1901; the *Heather*, 1949; and the *Collins New Classics*, 1947–54. The *World's Classics* edition of *Wuthering Heights*, 1930, repr. 1950, was the first to use the *first* edition of the novel rather than the second edition of 1850 in which Charlotte had altered some of the punctuation. Several of the novels are also available in *Penguin, Everyman* and other inexpensive editions.

Emily Brontë's *Poems* have been edited by Clement Shorter, London, 1910; by C. W. Hatfield, New York and London, 1941, repr. 1961; and by Philip Henderson, London, 1951. Charlotte Brontë's *Poems* were edited by Clement Shorter, with bibliography and notes by C. W. Hatfield, London, 1923.

LETTERS AND BIOGRAPHY

E. F. Benson. *Charlotte Brontë*. London, 1932. (Anti-Charlotte.)
E. C. Gaskell. *The Life of Charlotte Brontë*. London, 1857.
(Still a classic study.)
Winifred Gérin. *Charlotte Brontë The Evolution of Genius*. Oxford, 1967. (A fresh and scholarly interpretation of Charlotte's life and of her growth as a novelist.)
Lawrence and E. M. Hanson. *The Four Brontës*. London, 1949.
(Comprehensive and reliable.)
Margaret Lane. *The Brontë Story: A Reconsideration of Mrs Gaskell's Life of Charlotte Brontë*. London, 1948, repr. 1953.
(Very good indeed.)
Clement Shorter. *The Brontës' Life and Letters*. 2 vols. London, 1908.
May Sinclair. *The Three Brontës*. London, 1912.
(Still very readable and helpful.)
Muriel Spark (ed.). *The Brontë Letters*. London, 1954, repr. 1967.
T. J. Wise, and J. A. Symington. *The Brontës: Their Lives, Friendships and Correspondence*. 4 vols. Oxford, 1932.

STUDIES OF THE BRONTË JUVENILIA

Laura Hinkley. *The Brontës: Charlotte and Emily*. London, 1947. (See especially the appendix. Laura Hinkley's interpretation of the

Gondal Saga differs at certain important points from Fannie Ratch-ford's.)

Fannie Ratchford. *The Brontës' Web of Childhood*. New York, 1941.

Fannie Ratchford. *Gondal's Queen*. Austin, Texas, and Edinburgh, 1955. (This book gives a detailed reconstruction of the Gondal Saga with Emily Brontë's poems inserted at the appropriate places.)

CRITICAL STUDIES

(In *addition* to those books and essays from which the extracts in this volume have been taken.)

Jacques Blondel. *Emily Brontë: Expérience Spirituelle et Création Poétique*. Publ. de la Fac. des Lettres de l'Univ. de Clermont, Paris, 1963. (Sensitive and detailed. Includes the only serious critical study of the poems.)

Richard Chase. 'The Brontës: A Centennial Observance.' *Kenyon Review*, vol. IX, No. 4, 1947, pp. 487–506. (A well-known but much overrated article that takes a psychological approach to the novels.)

Philip Drew. 'Charlotte Brontë as a Critic of *Wuthering Heights*.' *Nineteenth Century Fiction*, vol. XVIII, No. 4, 1964, pp. 365–81.

Inga-Stina Ewbank. *Their Proper Sphere: A Study of the Brontë Sisters as Early Victorian Female Novelists*. London, 1966.

James Hafley. 'The Villain in *Wuthering Heights*.' *Nineteenth Century Fiction*, vol. XIII, No. 3, 1958, pp. 199–215. (Argues that Nelly is the real villain. Not finally convincing but worth considering.)

R. B. Heilman. 'Charlotte Brontë, Reason and the Moon.' *Nineteenth Century Fiction*, vol. XIV, No. 4, 1960, pp. 283–302.

Arnold Kettle. *An Introduction to the English Novel*. vol. I, London, 1951. Chapter V, pp. 139–55. (A Marxist approach to *Wuthering Heights*.)

G. D. Klingopulos. 'The Novel as Dramatic Poem: *Wuthering Heights*', *Scrutiny*, vol. XIV, No. 4, 1947, pp. 269–86.

Jacob Korg. 'The Problem of Unity in *Shirley*.' *Nineteenth Century Fiction*, vol. XII, No. 2, 1957, pp. 125–36.

R. B. Martin. *The Accents of Persuasion: Charlotte Brontë's Novels*. London, 1966.

M. H. Scargill. 'All Passion Spent: A Reconsideration of *Jane Eyre*.' *University of Toronto Quarterly*, vol. XIX, No. 2, 1950, pp. 120–5. (Oversimplifies the issues but is useful on the poetic symbolism in *Jane Eyre*.)